CONTENTS

DEAR READER

I am opening my heart and soul writing this account, even sharing excerpts from my journal. Please be kind. You may not agree with all of it; your path may differ, and that's okay. If there's anything I've learned, it's that we all have a unique trail to run in life, and it never looks like what we mapped out or expected.

I'm writing this because I was in a dark place for so long, and it almost cost my life. For many years, I struggled with deep depression, trying to pick up the pieces after devastating life events. I learned I can be in peak physical health, and at the same time, my mind is trying to kill me. Looking around, I know many others are also walking through those dark canyons. If you're not struggling yourself, you likely know someone who is and can help. I am sharing the paths we found to healing. There is no one-size-fits-all in life, especially not in mental health. However, psychedelics are a powerful medicine, able to promote health and growth in the deepest parts of our being.

For those who are concerned the use of psychedelics may conflict with their faith, please know these medicines will only enhance and strengthen your faith. Above all, psychedelics emphasize Love.

Here is my journey back to light and life.

With Love,
Byrd

A QUICK NOTE FROM THE AUTHORS

While this is a guide to psychedelics, it is also our story. As such, our chapters on the different psychedelics are the order in which each medicine entered our lives as we share our accounts. We started slow, with a natural source (mushrooms) first before trying anything synthetic (MDMA or LSD). We avoided substances with addictive potential. We continued adventuring based on our unique needs and stages of healing. That said, we are not placing chapters as a guide for progression but as information on each substance.

If you only read one chapter in this book, you should read MDMA: A Desert Trip Changed Our Lives (our favorite!). MDMA is the most powerful tool for couples to build strong bonds and establish healthy patterns of communication and conflict resolution. It is our favorite medicine and has significantly contributed to the success of our love story.

If you stay for a second chapter, read LSD: Couples That Trip Together Stay Together. As a versatile and fun substance, LSD is our second favorite. It complements MDMA and enhances music at concerts, festivals, and at home. LSD also gives you an incredible feeling of being connected to the people and world around you, a feeling often missing in modern times. Don't be intimidated; LSD received an ill-founded reputation from the war on drugs, but at the doses we discuss, acid is a predictable, safe, and beneficial drug.

Thank you for reading our story, and we hope you and your partner use the information here to connect, heal, and bond like never before!

Love ~ Les & Byrd

LEGAL DISCLAIMER

ABOUT THE AUTHORS

Les and Byrd are two RNs with over 20 years of combined mental health experience. Les has a master's in nursing education, and Byrd has a master's in nursing leadership and is a Board Certified Psychiatric and Mental Health RN. After losing a brother to suicide early in his career, Les dedicated himself to mental health, specializing in adolescent and adult psychiatric inpatient settings and substance abuse treatment. Byrd has professional and personal experience in mental health, diagnosed with Major Depressive Disorder, Generalized Anxiety Disorder, and PTSD as a survivor of domestic violence. Byrd has worked extensively with teens, adults, and Veterans in mental health and recovery from addiction. After significant struggles with depression, Byrd and Les began exploring psychedelics as a method to improve mental health and also became a resource for others seeking healing in this space. This book is their personal story of healing while also providing a guide for others interested in independently exploring psychedelics.

PRESCRIBING CHANGE: HOW 2 RNS FOUND A CALLING IN PSYCHEDELICS

They say great change is preceded by chaos. [63] I (Byrd) started my psychedelic journey as a result of great internal struggle and a history of trauma, which left me in a place of overwhelming depression. I spent so many years living in survival mode I no longer felt comfortable when life wasn't in crisis. When I finally decided to give psychedelics a try, I had struggled with depression for over 13 years. My symptoms slowly worsened, and other methods I tried, such as therapy, diet, exercise, and medication, were helpful but just not enough. The more things I tried, and the longer I attempted to manage how I felt, the more hopeless I felt. Understanding how I arrived at this juncture, willing to try *anything* to find healing, requires revisiting the journey that shaped my path.

I grew up a complete teetotaler. I was 37 before I tried my first alcoholic drink. *(Wine tasting with Les, go figure!)*. I have never smoked a single cigarette. I tried marijuana for the first time when I was 36, eating a gummy in hopes it would help with symptoms of depression and anxiety. *(And proceeded to throw up for hours -ugh!)* Ask anyone who knew me, and they would have voted me least likely to try a psychedelic substance---ever.

I was raised in a loving family. My mom gave birth to me at 21. A year later, she was pregnant with my brother and facing life as a single mom with two kids when someone knocked on her door and told her about Jesus. She became a Christian, started attending church, and met the man who would marry her and adopt my brother and me. Together, they had two more boys and raised all 4 of us in a strict fundamentalist, evangelical, non-denominational Christian fellowship. We went to church three times a week, prayer every morning, outreach once or twice a week, bible studies, and often revival (church every night for a week).

My dad was a pastor for a while when I was a kid. We didn't watch movies, never owned a TV, rarely listened to secular music, and closely filtered every part of our lives through Christian values. I was 10 when I became born again and 11 when I stood up at a youth service and said God called me to be a pastor's wife. I loved reading and began reading the Bible from cover to cover once a year, starting at 12. When we weren't in church, we were spending time with people in church.

The first time I thought about killing myself, I was 13. It's challenging to explain why my emotions strayed towards darkness, occasionally at first and overwhelmingly later. I had a happy childhood and a stable family life after my parents married and my dad adopted me. Research shows an interaction of genetic and environmental triggers causes depression. [64] Looking back at these thoughts and feelings at such a young age, it seems the genetic piece was there all along. The experiences over the years ahead would contribute to the environmental pieces. As I grew older, I was able to identify family members on both sides who had struggled with depression, anxiety, and substance abuse.

I tested into the gifted program in 3rd grade, earning top grades and awards for educational excellence throughout school. I graduated at 16, and the same year, I met a young man in church who was studying to be a pastor. Six days after I turned 18, we married. My first kiss ever was at the altar on our wedding day. Our daughter was born when I was 19, and our son when I was 21. The life I felt destined to live was marrying young, raising a family, and preaching the gospel by starting churches in new places. That version of my life didn't happen. Instead of becoming a pastor, he became an angry alcoholic.

The warning signs were there all along. He was arrested for drunk and disorderly conduct at 21 before joining the church and was easily angered, even when we were dating. However, I learned at a young age to distrust my deepest self as "feelings" come and go and instead obey what pastors and the church told me. There were strong beliefs that when someone becomes a Christian, they are a new person; who they were before becoming a Christian no longer matters because that isn't who they are now. Even if someone struggles with specific issues, Jesus can make them better. All you need for a marriage is love, forgiveness, and Jesus. Right?

The kids and I lived through a decade of increasingly worse abuse, trauma, and black nights of the soul. A good Christian wife is submissive, praying for her husband and maintaining strict confidence about troubles at home. I felt so trapped and broken; my kids were my only reason for continuing. He threatened if I left, he would take the kids and disappear. He told me I wouldn't be able to stop him from hurting the kids if I left and he had them alone. One terrible night, a SWAT team came and arrested him, and genuinely terrified, I filed for a restraining order.

I had entered nursing school before his arrest and spent the last year before graduation dividing my time and energy between the demands of school, a felony trial for domestic violence, and a divorce. When I wanted to drop out, my mother insisted I finish nursing school at any cost, and the kids and I moved in with my parents for two years. I graduated with my RN less than a month after my divorce, placing at the top of my class and testing into the top 1% of nursing students in the US with my exit exam scores while receiving my class's top award for Excellence in Leadership and Nursing.

As a nurse, I found my passion in working with pregnant teens at a local non-profit. We did everything from free pregnancy testing and options counseling to birthing and parenting classes. We worked with each teen mom until her baby turned two years old, visiting new moms at home and in the hospital. I traveled all over the county doing home visits, classes, and program outreach, often on my sport bike.

I tried to move on from the earlier years, but the dark emotions persisted. I had developed trauma superpowers such as the ability to dissociate, sometimes feeling entirely out of my body or unable to hear or mentally process things people said if there were negative or intense emotions involved. I struggled to speak if a situation was tense or conflict was involved, even at work. The kids and I had crazy startle reflexes *(friends said I was entertaining to watch movies with!)*. I had a strong intolerance for the smell of alcohol, particularly coming from anyone male. Certain situations made me highly uncomfortable, and I would find myself physically agitated, unable to sit down or physically relax until the feelings passed. Over time, the fight or flight symptoms, sleep issues, guilt, hopelessness, and depression grew worse.

I slowly transitioned away from the church I grew up in, unable to maintain the intensity of fundamentalist Christianity while also deeply loving and caring about broken people. The final breaking point was seeing a couple of pregnant teens I was close to kicked out of the church for what leadership deemed moral failings. I remember standing in the back of the church holding one of the teen moms' babies while the pastor preached about the importance of judging sin and, by extension, people who sin. In my heart, I knew I could love people and forgive hard things, but I didn't have it in me to judge others harshly.

My life was too broken to meet the expectations presented as requirements of faith, and the kids and I began attending another local church.

It's difficult to relate how deeply this affected my psyche. I believed attending the church I grew up in was the only way to Heaven; my eternal salvation depended on it. People in other churches might (*slim chance and only in select exceptions*) go to Heaven, but a truly committed Christian would be in that church. I felt supported by those in this church through the years of abuse, divorce, and single mom years after. Friends prayed for us, cried with us, and helped with the kids. I will never forget the first Christmas Eve we spent as a broken family, and ten people showed up at our door to sing Christmas carols and give us Christmas gifts. Up to that point, this church and its people were everything to us our whole lives.

Yet I struggled with the cognitive dissonance that this belief system gave my abuser all the tools to justify his behavior: a feeling of superiority as a man, a tyrant with ultimate control as the head of the house. I had to submit, even when he was making questionable decisions. We were secretive about issues in the home. Seeking help from those outside the church, even licensed counselors, was strongly discouraged. Any relationships, including family, outside the church were discouraged. Those who left were often cut off as negative influences, even by their immediate family. Moral failings were judged and punished with intense social consequences (loss of ministry, decreased status, being kicked out of the church, etc.). As a result, openness and honesty were discouraged by default. Struggles were buried until circumstances were so overwhelming we couldn't pretend everything was okay anymore. As a culture, actual abuse was hidden, and victims were instructed to forgive no matter the offense or how often. After all, Jesus told Peter to forgive other's sins up to seventy times seven. [Matthew18:21-25] As victims, we *must* forgive because our eternal destination depends on it; if we don't forgive others, then Jesus won't forgive us. Over and over, women were taught to submit, be circumspect, pray for their husbands quietly, and guarantee to have regular sex. [54] Scripture justified all of these beliefs. I was distrustful of anything and everyone outside the church.

In addition, the visceral and truly terrifying fear of Hell was pounded into us from a young age. We believed the fear of the Lord was the beginning of knowledge. You can't worship and love God until you fear Him. I was taught people have to be lost before they can be found and need to be told they are sinners going to Hell before they hear about the love and forgiveness of Jesus on the cross. Hell was something real and horrible beyond imagination. We were born sinners, and at any moment, we could die, and if we weren't right with God, we would go straight to Hell. Every service, multiple times a week, we were asked if we died tonight, would we go to Heaven or Hell? I heard pastors laugh about a kid who grew up and left the church and was terrified to sleep with a heating blanket for fear of being electrocuted in their sleep because then they would die and go to Hell. They said the kids who grew up in the church couldn't get away from the fear of Hell.

I remember biting my nails as a child and then literally praying to repent, terrified I had disobeyed my parents and was now going to Hell. We watched rated-R movies on Hell and produced Haunted Houses yearly depicting Hell and demons. In addition to Hell, there was a lot of preaching on the imminent Rapture. At any moment, Jesus might come back, and if you were in any way sinning, you would be left behind to face an apocalyptic world. Perhaps because I was a people pleaser by nature, rating high in Agreeableness and Conscientiousness (Type A), it affected me more deeply than others.

I lived my life truly terrified to do anything God would consider a sin, even a little. I grew up repenting throughout the day, every day, never realizing how deeply my psyche had been affected. I couldn't understand why I struggled so much with deep feelings of rejection and self-hatred.

Leaving the church cost me most of my lifelong friends and our support system. It would be a long time down the road, after innumerable sessions of Eye Movement Desensitization and Reprocessing (EMDR) therapy, before I began to sort out the connections between the abuse we survived, the church we attended, the beliefs I was raised with, and my faith.

Thankfully, though my parents still attended the same church as before, they continued to love and support us, functioning as a vital part of our lives. Their love and help got us through many difficult moments. Innumerable times, they picked the kids up after school, helped with homework, volunteered at the school, offered wisdom and advice, and provided financial assistance. They were there for it all.

The non-profit for pregnant teens was grant-based and eventually lost funding, closing in our area. I cried while packing up the office; to this day, that was my favorite position as an RN, my passion and niche. I transitioned to another position as an RN, working with first-time moms of all ages throughout our rural county, and started classes for my bachelor's degree. I received a prestigious national scholarship, covering up to $30,000 of classes yearly for two years. Because of this incredible generosity, I attained my BSN, even as a single mom. I am still awed by their kindness; this was a bright spot during some darker moments.

After two years of being single, I began dating again. Twice, I had short but serious relationships that ended in broken engagements. While I learned a lot, the emotional toll was heavy. *(No, really, what was I thinking?!)* The losses finally caught up with me in an overwhelming ocean of emotions. I was drowning. A coworker overheard me trying and failing to hold it together, crying quietly in my cubicle at work. She referred me to free counseling via a local support program for survivors of domestic violence. They saved my life the first time. I slowly began putting the pieces of myself back together. I continued therapy off and on for years as needed.

After a few years, I remarried and began working in mental health. I became a board-certified psychiatric and mental health RN. I love being a nurse and helping others. In every position, I threw myself into improving systems and processes and healing people. I have a gift for seeing the potential in every person, department, position, and facility. On the other hand, I grieve the wasted potential in people and our society.

My ex was placed on supervised visitation, eventually progressing to one weekend a month of unsupervised visitation with the kids. Unfortunately, family court allows abusers to continue causing emotional turmoil and trauma. My ex and his mother took me to court five times in ten years (grandparents have the right to take parents to court separately in our state). I endured two inappropriate and retaliative state Department of Child Safety (DCS) investigations. *(All accusations unsubstantiated.)* The police responded to multiple complaints against me, randomly showing up at the house for reasons such as the kids not calling their dad to check in for a single night. On the other hand, he would randomly stop his visitation with the kids for months at a time.

Abusers will use every minuscule avenue of control available when a situation is out of their control. I was forced to send the kids on visits even when they were screaming and crying because they didn't want to go. To this day, my kids and I are working through their resentments and feelings of abandonment that I wasn't there for them when they needed me and that I made them go and didn't protect them. He failed to pay child support for years, racking up over $21,000 in child support debt while still taking me to court repeatedly. It's impossible to put the constant pressure, scrutiny, criticism, and ongoing legal actions into words.

The heart and soul tear into pieces, sending the little people who mean more than anything to you off with the person who terrifies you more than anything. My soul was bleeding out with thousands of cuts over decades. The stress was unbelievable, and my desire to do what was best for my kids was the only thing that kept me going. Both of my children struggled with suicidal ideation and depression as they became teens. I began long-distance running as a way to cope with depression, running in the forest for hours, praying, and seeking peace.

My second marriage failed after six years. Looking back, I can see the pressure caused by the ongoing legal issues, the kids and I struggling with trauma responses. I made decisions from a place of woundedness instead of healing and strength. I almost lost my faith after a decade in an abusive Christian marriage the first time I divorced. I was eventually able to rationalize that God gives us free will, and sometimes people use free will to sin, and that doesn't mean God wanted those things to happen to us. I remarried another Christian, and now, I was at a complete loss. I tried again and failed. I was in deep depression, and everything I thought I believed broke into pieces. I was irreparably damaged inside.

Both times I married, we didn't live together before the wedding because sex before marriage is a sin. Unfortunately, there are things you can't possibly know until you live together. I quickly realized I had made a mistake, but I also knew divorce was a sin. I was determined to make it work; after all, I gave my word, and Christians don't get divorced. My kids needed stability. By sheer force of will, I was determined to make this work. Our past trauma and disparate personalities triggered each other, and both of us were deeply depressed.

Eventually, I couldn't go on living the way I was, with no connection, desperately lonely. I knew divorce was a sin and I should stick it out no matter what; at the same time, I was feeling intense emotional pain, a complete failure in life, and deeply depressed. I felt my only options were divorce or suicide; maybe God would understand I had tried my best and couldn't measure up.

To distract myself from deepening depression, I threw myself into a self-paced master's program, completing my Master of Science in Nursing (MSN) degree in 4 months with honors. Even as a psychiatric RN, I couldn't accept the idea of starting medications for depression. There is a stigma associated; something must be intrinsically wrong with your mind if you need drugs to cope. I was deeply concerned if I started medication, I wouldn't ever be able to stop. Given my past, I am terrified of addiction and fiercely independent. I tried every other method to address depression, including diet changes, exercise, therapy, lab work to rule out physiological causes, Vitamin D, staying active with projects and school, etc. A couple of close coworkers suggested alternative options for treating depression, such as psilocybin, and shared current applicable research. For the first time, I heard of psychedelics as a method to treat depression, but it was far from the last.

After running alone in the forest for years, a coworker invited me to join a local running group. Surprisingly, I learned people run daytime and nighttime in any weather and for days without stopping. Trail running kept me sane, giving me a safe place to work through emotions, an opportunity to challenge myself, and a way to release negative emotions. As my depression worsened, I found solace in long-distance running, which

eventually evolved into running ultra-marathons. My mom and sister-in-law joined me, becoming ultra-runners as well. *(To be transparent, as the longest distance I have completed in an event is 92 kilometers or 57 miles, I still consider myself a baby ultra-runner!)*

The ultra-marathon community embodies kindness and acceptance for each other, allowing everyone to run their race to the best of their capabilities, accepting that runners come in all stages of life. *(Forward is a pace!)* Pushing my body beyond what I thought was possible, relying on my mind long past when my body was done, and maintaining incredible mental discipline helped me learn I was capable of much more than I thought. I grew in confidence and independence, with so many possibilities open before me.

Despite the miles, the depression continued to pursue me. I realized I had reached an awful place one day when I woke up wanting to kill myself, ran over 27 miles with more than 5000 feet of elevation gain, came home exhausted, and still wanted to die. I couldn't outrun this darkness no matter how hard I tried and how far I ran.

Given my upbringing, I was terrified if I killed myself, I would go straight to Hell. I believed that suicide is self-murder and killing myself was a straight path to Hell. The terror of Hell was pounded into the deepest part of my soul. One was always one sin away from dying unexpectedly and ending up in Hell. On the other hand, I believed God is a God of love, grace, and mercy, and maybe I should give up, cast myself onto His perfect nature, and trust that He would sort it out on the other side. Being all-knowing, He is the One who could see everything, every wound, all the pain, and how hard I tried.

This terror of Hell kept me from killing myself many times and would come up again and again as I tried to heal through psychedelics, sometimes in a very high-risk way. I talked to a pastor from a different local church, asking if God sends people to Hell if they kill themselves. He explained suicide is like someone dying of cancer; the person has lost their battle with depression, and this isn't a choice to sin, resulting in someone going to Hell. I realized as a nurse, if a patient came in with an infection or anything treatable by medication, we would quickly and easily start a prescription, and they would recover. Why was I hesitating taking medication for mental health?

I started Eye Movement Desensitization and Reprocessing (EMDR) and, unsurprisingly, was diagnosed with Major Depressive Disorder (MDD.), Post Traumatic Stress Disorder (PTSD), and General Anxiety Disorder (GAD). EMDR is a psychotherapy treatment specifically designed to treat survivors of trauma. Patients practice a method of bilateral stimulation, such as moving the eyes left to right, or a tactile sensation, such as vibration alternating between left and right hands. While experiencing bilateral stimulation, the patient reprocesses traumatic memories. The brain tends to store trauma on one side of the brain. Reprocessing with bilateral stimulation allows the mind to use both sides of the brain while remembering and thus reduce the vividness and emotions associated with the memories.

In addition, the therapist guides you through identifying negative beliefs about yourself and the world associated with trauma. Many people experience traumatic events, but not everyone who survives trauma develops PTSD. One of the differences is when trauma breaks your worldview, causing you to internalize negative beliefs about yourself and the world. EMDR allows you to identify those negative and crippling beliefs and replace them with accurate and balanced beliefs.

EMDR is incredibly effective. Sitting in the therapist's office the first time, feeling like I wanted to die so badly every day, I didn't even know anymore why I was sad. I was at the bottom of a mountain of emotion and could see no way to dig myself out. I couldn't sort out where my feelings about one thing started or another ended. Everything just blended and churned. I was so tired in my soul. It was exhausting and challenging work, and sometimes, I had to force myself to make the drive to an appointment. My therapist was compassionate and always on the alert to stop if a session became too overwhelming.

She asked me two vital questions. What made me happy in the past year? What did I, Byrd, want to do? Not what *should* I do, or what do *others* want me to do. What did *I* want to do? She had me draw symbols for what my life was like now, and on the other side of the page, symbols for what I would like to see in my life if anything was possible. Then, she asked me to draw a bridge between the two and add symbols over the bridge for what would have to change to get from one side to the other. It felt impossible to bridge the gap from where I was now to where I would like to be.

The thoughts of suicide grew worse as the cognitive dissonance inside heightened. I was a Christian, but I was drowning in depression. What was wrong with me? The thoughts became so pressing I had to chant to stop myself from acting on it. I had a plan and access to my preferred method. In desperation, I asked to be referred to a psychiatric provider to start medication. She saved my life yet again, developing a regimen that allowed me to sleep. We initiated a medication trial while waiting for my genetic testing results to point us in the right direction for the most effective antidepressant medications. I filed for leave approval in advance under the Family Medical Leave Act (FMLA) at work. Every day, I wondered if I would be able to drag myself out of bed again, yet I didn't want to lose my job in the event I ended up in an inpatient psychiatric ward.

It would take four medications before finding one that worked well overall. Right away, the first medication gave me the mental space to take a step back from the overwhelming, pressuring thoughts of suicide. Unfortunately, despite the medication, the depression persisted, causing emotional pain that manifested as physical chest discomfort day in and day out. My heart hurt palpably. The second medication made me so tired I could sleep all day, literally spending 21 hours in bed on my days off. Maybe my mind needed the rest and an escape. The third medication made me nauseous, and I lost 7 pounds in 2 weeks and could barely run. The fourth medication gave me the energy I needed to burn my life down.

My grandmother died. She was my closest relative and had been for decades. I told her everything. She couldn't understand why I was depressed, pointing out I had so much good in my life. She remembered her mother had been "emotionally weak" and "had a couple of breakdowns and had to go back to the family ranch in Mexico to recover." Yet, in her traditional homesteading mindset, people should pull up their bootstraps and keep moving forward, no matter what life throws at them. It is what it is. I couldn't understand how I felt either. What was wrong with me? Neither of us understood the long-term physiological effects of trauma.

I sat there in her house the day after she died, trying to decide if I should get a divorce or kill myself. I kept thinking about what a close friend and coworker said: Maybe if I gave my life more time and continued living, someday it would all make sense. I could beg God for forgiveness. Suicide and divorce are both sins – which one was worse? At least if I continued living, there was time for all this chaos to make sense.

With that slim hope in mind, I filed for divorce, sold our house, agreed to provide him with 60% as an apology for calling it quits, and moved into my car. I didn't know what to do, but I knew I couldn't continue as I was. I had to lay down many burdens I had been carrying to start figuring it all out. I was overwhelmed and exhausted in every way:

body, mind, and soul. Eventually, I found a condo, and my living circumstances stabilized again.

A friend and coworker recommended I read "How to Change Your Mind" by Michael Pollen. I listened to the book while running an unofficial ultra to the bottom of the Grand Canyon, up to Ribbon Falls, and back up to the South Rim. I was so intrigued by the idea that I could reset my neural networks, develop neuroplasticity, and maybe give my brain a fresh start. I was convinced I had burned through *a lot of* neurotransmitters in the past couple of decades. *(For more on neuroplasticity please refer to the chapter titled "Neuroplasticity and the Science Behind Psychedelics.")*

We discussed the risk of addiction at length. After researching and talking to others who had taken mushrooms, I confirmed there was no chance of addiction. The neurotransmitters impacted by mushrooms need time to reset, rendering repeat doses close together ineffective. People who had self-administered doses of mushrooms close together reported decreasing and then no effect within a couple of weeks. Given previous life experiences, this was a huge relief.

I had tried a lot of other things and still struggled every day, drowning in an ocean of darkness. Some days, I was treading water, and my head was just above the waves; others, I sank down and could barely breathe. I felt hope with the process I had started in EMDR and decided to experiment with mushrooms to see if I could heal my mind. *(And seeing as I love plants, why not grow some?)* Les and I transitioned from close friends and coworkers to lovers during this time. We decided to grow some mushrooms and see if that would make a difference in our mental health.

THE 3 S's OF TRIPPING: SET, SETTING, AND SURRENDER

One's environment and mental mindset significantly affect their experience while on a psychedelic. Set is an overarching description of the person's mindset going into the experience, including mood, thoughts, expectations, and stated intentions. Setting refers to the person's physical and social environment during the event. In his book, "How to Change Your Mind," author Michael Pollan attributes the idea of set and setting to Al Hubbard, who learned the concept while studying the use of psychedelic mushrooms in Mexico. Timothy Leary, one of the fathers of modern psychedelics, popularized the term in the 1960s. Historically, in many indigenous cultures' psychedelics were administered in elaborate rituals with particular set and setting practices that continue today in many parts of the world.

As psychedelics such as LSD gained popularity in the 1950s, two very different sets and settings were researched, with wildly divergent outcomes. Early research around LSD focused on studying mental illness, referring to LSD as a psychomimetic inducing temporary insanity. Patients in mental institutions were given LSD, often with little or no choice in the matter. These patients were poorly prepared and even told to expect a "few hours of madness" without mention of positive benefits or setting positive intentions. Some of the patients were restrained. The setting was typically a hospital environment with fluorescent lights, uncomfortable seating, and endless questions and psychometric testing accompanying experiences. Impersonal psychiatrists and staff surrounded the patients. In the aftermath, the patients were left alone without peers and no mental framework to interpret the experience and thus were often unable to integrate the experience. These patients primarily reported negative experiences and outcomes, with the psychiatrists describing the medication as "essentially anxiety-producing agents" and noting none of the patients wanted to retake LSD. Sadly, many of these experiences led to much of the misunderstanding surrounding the use of psychedelics, a stigma that remains in Western culture today. [18]

Conversely, another group of researchers approached LSD as a therapeutic agent, able to produce "cognitive enhancement" and "consciousness expansion." Participants were students and professionals who volunteered for the experiences. These individuals received thorough preparation and were told to expect positive and possibly life-changing outcomes. This research took place in a comfortable environment, with sofas, pillows, and the ability to recline. Participants were able to listen to music. Socially, the setting was supportive, with participants often engaging with friends during and after the experience. Individuals were given a mental framework to interpret the encounter. Little surprise, this group reported overall positive experiences and outcomes. [18]

A study published in 2021 found that individuals who rated high in openness, absorption (openness to diverse cognitive and imaginative experiences), acceptance, and a state of surrender were more likely to have a positive and mystical-type experience while under the influence of a psychedelic. Participants who rated low in these traits or presented in a preoccupied, apprehensive, or confused state were more likely to experience acute adverse reactions. [19]

Understandably, adequate preparation and support during a psychedelic experience affect the outcome as well. Cultures across the world combine the use of psychedelics with specific ceremonies, songs, and rituals to achieve healing for the mind, body, and soul. Often, these traditions have been developed over thousands of years and handed down from generation to generation of ancestors.

In contemporary medical settings, practitioners seek to create an environment that is as comfortable as possible, often replicating home environments in medical offices to enhance relaxation. Typically, research trials with psychedelics involve two therapists/guides for support, music via headphones, dim lighting, and eye masks to block light. One study of participants using Dimethyltryptamine (DMT) found improved experiences when participants selected music, underwent a medical screening, and identified an emergency contact. [19]

A couple exploring psychedelics should mindfully select their preferred location for the experience. Many substances, such as Ecstasy (aka methylenedioxymethamphetamine or

MDMA), are known for enhancing shows and parties. On the other hand, home rolling is when a couple shares the experience at home, usually alone.

Our favorite approach for ourselves and other couples is home rolling. Home rolling allows a couple to disconnect from all external distractions and focus on each other, with enhanced effects. In the quieter, less visually stimulating home setting, the experience shared between a couple differs from what is described by those partying. In fact, with MDMA in particular, we commit to taking this only with each other, alone by ourselves. This medicine changed our lives and holds a sacred place in our relationship.

Couples should consider aspects such as temperature and physical comfort. We love being outdoors; however, when temperatures are freezing outside, we choose locations that offer a warm and cozy indoor alternative. Psychedelics tend to dilate the pupils, so dimly lit areas or waiting until the sun goes down are often preferred. We love the enhanced star gazing while on psychedelics! After we began using psychedelics, I suddenly understood why black lights and neon gear were all the rage. You will not be moving around much, so it's essential to have comfortable furnishings such as a bed, couch, pillows, soft blankets, etc.

Don't forget food! Psychedelics increase neuroplasticity, and something you eat might taste like heaven in your mouth. Depending on your constitution, you may go long periods without wanting to eat. Sometimes, you may feel nauseous and want something light. Either way, you probably won't take time out to go grocery shopping, and special foods enhance the experience. We developed specific snacks and drinks we included during our experiences. In addition, some psychedelics can affect your fluid and electrolyte balance, so it's important to have liquids on hand to drink as much as possible. We also include one or two bottles of electrolytes such as Liquid I.V. Balanced electrolytes help with any symptoms of dehydration that may arise and decrease overall fatigue after long hours of fun.

Music is often an incredible part of psychedelic experiences. Over time, we developed a playlist for our special nights. We created another for the incredibly sexy nights. Later, we developed a playlist with friends while enjoying psychedelics as a group *(After all, friends who trip together stay together!)* We listen to our favorite songs on repeat and add more as the mood strikes. Later, we can play one of these songs, and the fantastic memories and feelings will all come flooding back. You have never really heard music until you've heard music on LSD.

An individual's expectations and mood immediately before taking a psychedelic will affect the overall event. Those who approach the medicine with openness and a positive mindset have better outcomes and benefit more. Conversely, those who approach the occasion with a negative mindset or are in an unstable mood are more likely to experience adverse effects or have a challenging trip. [20]

Intentions are powerful. The mind is able and willing to heal itself. Starting every experience by stating intentions points the mind in the right direction. Some choose to ask their mind questions such as, "What do I need to feel peace?" Others state their intentions as if they have already achieved the desired state, "I feel peace" or "I sleep through the night without nightmares." For couples, the intention may be shared, such as, "We are closer than ever." "Our connection is deep and secure." "We only speak truth and love to each other." "Our souls are open, vulnerable, and safe with one another." Intentions allow your mind to support your desires from within, giving your mind a compass and direction to follow.

Intentions should be part of a larger goal. For example: To improve your relationship. Intentions are always a positive affirmation. *(We have enough negativity going on in and around us already!)* Intentions should be part of a more extensive ritual, often occurring regularly. In this case, stating the intention is a step in the ritual of exploring psychedelics together and should happen as you begin the experience. The period between self-administering the psychedelic and waiting for the effects to start is an ideal time to state intentions. Sharing these statements out loud with each other begins the process of opening our hearts to one another. [21]

One has to be able to let go or remain in a state of surrender as feelings and sensations arise during a psychedelic experience. Many depictions describe participants experiencing a "bad" or "challenging" trip if the individual fights the feelings, thoughts, and sensations. Surrender is the willful release of one's goals, constructs, habits, and preferences. Surrender can even be the release of oneself, letting go completely. Researchers found that surrender was positively associated with spiritual change, ego-dissolution, mystical-type experiences, and long-term positive change. On the other hand, surrender decreased experiences of acute dread and long-term negative change. [20]

A considerable component of set and setting involves the social aspects. We cannot overstate the importance of who is around you when you are exploring psychedelics. In a coupleship, being with a psychologically safe partner is particularly important. When I was in an abusive relationship, everything I confided in a moment of trust and openness was later used against me in as psychologically devastating a manner as possible. I cannot imagine how much more damaging it would have been if I had opened myself up even further and deeper with the use of psychedelics. Over the years, I developed internal barriers to protect my mind and heart, which were necessary for my safety and security.

In no way would it have been advisable for me to prompt enhanced openness and connection while in this relationship. With this in mind, psychedelics should be used with caution, especially if there is any hint of abuse in your relationship, whether that is mental, emotional, sexual, or physical. Ever. If your partner has been abusive, strongly consider other methods to grow your relationship or seek out a trained relationship therapist before moving forward. In my situation, what I said in the safety of a therapist's office would have been later twisted and used to hurt me when we were alone.

I would have done anything to save our marriage and gave too much of myself as it was. I was conditioned to react to my former partner by feeling sorry for him and considering his emotions and needs above mine. Even profoundly hurt, I continually sought to heal our relationship and was on high alert for anything that would upset him, regardless of how I felt or my needs. I am so grateful I did not know about psychedelics, as I can only imagine the more profound damage this medicine could have caused.

Ask yourself if your partner is safe to be open with before proceeding. Psychedelics are potent medicines and allow direct access to the mind, heart, and soul. These should be used with extreme caution if abuse is a concern. These same considerations apply if you branch out and include other friends in your experiences.

Finally, do not forget your physical health. Each of these is a medicine and has distinct effects on the body. Not everyone is in a state physically, mentally, or emotionally to explore psychedelics. If you have any concerns in one of these areas, seek out a professional before proceeding with caution.

Ask yourself the following questions:
(Note: This applies to both men and women.)

"Is your partner truly safe?"

"Are you confident nothing you share will be used against you later in a hurtful way?"

"Can you freely share your concerns, thoughts, and feelings with your partner without fear of how they will respond?"

"Is your relationship equal in power?"

"Is it possible to prioritize your own needs without fearing retaliation from your partner?"

"Is conflict safe in your relationship?"

"If you bring up something that has hurt you, does the other person truly hear you?" (Or is the situation turned around to where you did something wrong?)

If the answer to these questions is "No," **stop.** Consider an alternative way to grow your relationship, or contact a marriage counselor.

HOLDING SPACE FOR YOUR PARTNER

The therapeutic power of psychedelics, especially for couples, is primarily accomplished by talking through your experience with someone, hopefully, your partner. The supporting partner is *holding space* for the other. What is *holding space*? Has your partner ever been upset and just needed to vent? Your role was not to solve their problems but to listen compassionately and actively. You were holding space, which is easier for some than for others. One thing to keep in mind while holding space is that your partner is their own best healer. You don't need to fix anything. This doesn't mean you can check out and pull out your phone. No, you must be fully present and engaged.

Holding space can be simply listening while being present, engaged, and empathetic. Holding space can expand, as you grow, into something like therapy light. The more you understand the mind and soul, the more you can help during these moments. *Active listening* is helpful while holding space or interacting with friends, colleagues, loved ones, and partners.

If you want to take your space-holding game to the next level, we suggest reading "Introduction to Internal Family Systems" or "No Bad Parts" by Richard Schwartz, Ph .D. [49][50] Internal Family Systems (IFS) is a theoretical framework for understanding the complexity of human personality. Dr. Schwartz's theory states that our personality is many individual parts (subpersonalities) that interact with each other in functional and dysfunctional ways. [50] IFS can be challenging at times, but when coupled with MDMA, you can condense years of therapy into a night or two.

Les worked with an IFS therapist for a time and found the theory helpful but difficult. From this experience and learning more about the theory of IFS, Les has been able to incorporate IFS into psychedelic space holding to significant effect. Psychedelics allow you to get past your ego and easily access the dreamlike state necessary to do the work of IFS. But why IFS? Simple, IFS is a non-judgmental, largely self-directed, and simple framework to empower individuals to heal themselves. IFS allows individuals to heal themselves instead of relying on a guru or therapist to perform their healing.

If you don't consider yourself comfortable as a space holder, I suggest reading the guide and books above and looking within yourself. When we can't hold space for others, it is usually because parts of our personality are uncomfortable with the intimate vulnerability necessary to be with someone equally vulnerable. If you don't feel comfortable holding space but haven't tried while on MDMA, try it out on MDMA and see if that drops some of your barriers. Our use of psychedelics has shown us how to hold space and communicate better.

If you start with love, curiosity, and compassion in your heart, you are starting from a solid position.

NEUROPLASTICITY AND THE SCIENCE BEHIND PSYCHEDELICS

The benefits of psychedelic use, both in this book and published widely, are founded in solid science. Neuroplasticity is the brain's ability to grow, develop, change, and adapt across the lifespan. If you think of your brain as a system of wired electrical circuits, with each circuit representing a memory, function, or process within your brain, you will see that there needs to be a process to add new memories, skills, or functions to the brain. [53] The brain's ability to grow new circuits or to remove unused ones is neuroplasticity. This description is oversimplified, but you don't need to be a neuroscientist to get the gist here.

As an adult, those deeply established circuits are called the *Default Mode Network*. Your Default Mode Network is responsible for the automatic responses you have in life, both good and bad. If you find that criticism causes you to become angry and defensive without thinking, that's an example of your Default Mode Network at work. Your Default Mode Work is challenging to change since the circuits are more established than those that help you remember a phone number. To change the Default Mode Network, you need some help to boost your neuroplasticity.

Our brains learn and grow quickly during early development when our neuroplasticity is at its highest. The neuroplastic nature of our brains is why it is so easy for children under 5 to learn a foreign language; their brains can grow/learn fast enough to learn two languages without even realizing they are learning it. As we become adults and age, our neuroplasticity slows down, and we establish our Default Mode Network. Our brain can still grow new circuits and prune old ones. However, the rate is much slower than for a 5-year-old.

Another benefit of a young and plastic brain is the ability to heal from physical and psychological injuries to the brain and nervous system. Children's ability to repair, adapt, and change the circuits to regain function is more significant. More neuroplasticity is a good thing, right? Absolutely, but how do we get that? Meditation, exercise, and using your brain can increase neuroplasticity to a degree. We need to boost our neuroplasticity significantly to regain that child-like adaptability. Psychedelics can do this.

MDMA, ketamine, LSD, psilocybin, and other psychedelics can boost our neuroplasticity, accounting for part of their antidepressant and mental health improvement effects. [52] The research, hampered by the legality of psychedelics, is still emerging to nail down the specifics of how psychedelics improve neuroplasticity. However, the initial findings and known benefits of psychedelics show that their psychological benefits are, at least, partially attributed to increased neuroplasticity.

Psychedelics allow us to revert to the Play-Doh-like brains of our childhood and turn off our Default Mode Networks. So what? Well, if your brain can learn and unlearn better in the time during and after a psychedelic trip, you can use this time to dive into your psyche, bypass your default reactions in your Default Mode Network, and cut out old beliefs that no longer serve you and also add new beliefs. This phenomenon is what is driving psychedelic-assisted psychotherapy. Increasing your plasticity during therapy can accomplish months or years of work in a day or afternoon. The tall, complex barriers we have built over the years become soft and pliable, allowing you, a therapist, or your partner to assist you in rebuilding your mind into something that serves you better.

This lowering of barriers is also what contributes to the increased connection you will feel with your partner while using psychedelics like MDMA. Our Default Mode Network hampers our ability to connect deeply and address difficult memories or problems, but psychedelics allow us to turn off that network and create new connections. Imagine if that criticism you hear from your partner doesn't cause an immediate and adverse reaction, and you see that the comment was not a criticism at all but a plea from your partner's heart. This new approach would be life changing.

The Default Mode Network is responsible for feelings about the self as a separate entity and negative self-talk. The Default Mode Network is hyperactive in depressed individuals. Psychedelics decrease or even turn off the Default Mode Network, causing the sensation of self-dissolving (e.g., ego dissolution), stopping subconscious negative self-talk, and even decreasing inhibitions. Lowering the sense of self as a separate entity allows for enhanced connection with others and the world around us. In the case of ketamine, the Default Mode Network turns off completely and quickly, making ketamine a very effective substance in treating depression and suicidal ideation.

If you want to dive deeper into research and science, many videos, books, and articles on these aspects of psychedelics exist. This section was only to cover the very basics of how psychedelics work to heal your mind and relationships while also promoting deep connections. There are still mysteries surrounding the function of psychedelics, but what we know is enough to move forward with confidence that psychedelics can help across many domains.

PSILOCYBIN MUSHROOMS: THE FUNGUS INSIDE ME

Introduction

Psilocybin mushrooms, also known as magic mushrooms, boomers, shrooms, and mushies, are a family of mushrooms that grow in the wild and in closets worldwide. But these aren't your typical shiitakes. Psilocybin mushrooms are potent psychedelics. Shrooms come in wide varieties, but they all share the active ingredients of psilocybin and psilocin.

Every substance has a different energy or feel to it. Psilocybin mushrooms, except at low doses (under 2 grams), can feel more like medicine as they push you into your subconscious and work to heal you. Because of these introspective healing properties, your experiences as a couple with psilocybin may be more of healing and supporting each other as the medicine works through one or both of you rather than just for fun.

A brilliant shaman revealed a beautiful truth about plant medicines to me: You must consider the environment where the medicine lives to understand the nature of the medicine. Psilocybin spreads mainly below the surface and connects the many plants through their interaction with the roots. The deep, soil-diving nature of psilocybin provides insight into how it will dig into your body and spirit to connect and pull out what is inside you. The "darkness" of psilocybin (at high doses) results from digging deep into your soul and psyche like a fungus through the soil. Plant medicine is a full-spectrum medicine that has a spirit of its own. Each medicine is unique and will work within you differently.

History

The origins of psychedelic mushroom use go back to the times of the first humans and likely beyond. Archeologists have found rock art depicting psilocybin mushrooms as far back as 9000 BC. In 1957, Valentina and Gordon Wasson were the first Americans to participate in an indigenous mushroom ceremony. They published their experiences in Life Magazine, sharing this "new" substance with the world. Wasson's discovery did not take long to inspire a generation of hippies. By the 1960s, universities were conducting trials and exposing college students to increasing doses of psilocybin. [48]

The Marsh Chapel Experiment

On Good Friday, April 20, 1962, at the Boston University's Chapel, a shocking experiment would forever change the world. Timothy Leary and Richard Alpert, as part of the Harvard Psilocybin Project, gave a group of Divinity students large doses of psilocybin to see if religiously predisposed individuals would reliably have mystical experiences. *(And, oh boy, they did!)* Most of the students reported experiencing a profound religious experience as a result of the psilocybin. It was a very Good Friday for these young men. Unfortunately, Leary didn't have the proper approval to conduct the psilocybin experiment and was dismissed. Leary and Alpert went on to fuel much of the psychedelic revival during the 1960s and 1970s. [48]

It seems shocking to give conservative divinity students a heroic dose of psilocybin, but this experience forever changed these young men. (We'll discuss dosing below.) One of the students, Huston Smith, went on to publish many textbooks on comparative religion. Smith described his experience as "the most powerful cosmic homecoming I have ever experienced." [1] Psilocybin has remained a part of the American and European psychedelic tradition ever since.

Legal Status

Shrooms are found in the forests and fields of much of America and Europe and are easy to cultivate, making their prohibition extremely challenging. Prohibition did not stop the American government from trying. In 1968, the federal government made psilocybin mushrooms and synthetic psilocybin and psilocin Schedule 1 drugs under the Controlled Substances Act.

Schedule 1, repeated on these pages, is part of the government's attempt to classify the risk of various pharmaceutical, synthetic, and plant-based substances. Schedule 1 drugs are *supposedly* highly addictive and have no medicinal benefits. Unfortunately, the scheduling of drugs was never intended to be scientific and was used to fuel the War on Drugs. As a result of this scheduling, psilocybin mushrooms, and many other substances were instantly illegal. At the time, the government halted research on psilocybin and would not restart it for nearly 40 years.

Where does that leave us? Well, federally, psilocybin mushrooms are still very illegal. But, at the state level, we are starting to see bills that decriminalize shrooms. Also, the federal government allows research to continue despite their legal status. Check your local and state laws, but know that shrooms are still very illegal in the eyes of Uncle Sam. If you don't know where to find shrooms, learn how to grow them at home. *(I don't recommend foraging unless you really know your mushrooms.)* The supplies are readily available, and you can legally purchase shroom spores. Also, the mycologist community on the forums is constructive and supportive of new growers.

Be careful, but also know that shrooms are not the priority of local law enforcement. Their focus has shifted to fentanyl and methamphetamine.

Byrd's Story

It's a lot harder to grow psychedelic mushrooms than you would think. We love plants, and I am known for my green thumb, but mushrooms are sensitive little things. We bought the spores and, over months, grew them, following stringent sterile protocols to prevent contamination. Would you believe it's legal to buy all the supplies, including the spores, but not to grow the mushrooms? *(Weird world we live in).*

First, the spores are mixed with a sterile growing medium using a needle to inject the spores into a pre-sterilized bag of wheat berries without causing contamination. *(Those RN skills were coming in handy after all.)* The wheat berries are placed in a dark cupboard and checked occasionally. After about six weeks, the mycelium spreads throughout the wheat berries.

Next, the berries with the mycelium are mixed with cocoa coir and perlite. This mix is placed in a sterile container with a lid and carefully spritzed with water every few days until the mushrooms sprout. Once the mushrooms are fully grown, each one is gently harvested and dried. The dried mushrooms are eaten or blended in a drink.

After about three months, we had a crop with a few flushes of growth totaling nearly 26 grams of dried mushrooms to work with. We started with low doses as I had never taken any psychedelic substance before. *(My first-ever glass of wine was earlier this same year.)* The first dose of 0.5 grams didn't feel like much. I felt a little giggly, and we laughed a lot that afternoon. We tried 1 gram on a hike in the forest with friends, laughing and talking about our shared existential crisis.

One weekend, we planned to try 2 grams for the first time. That same week one of my daughter's closest friends was raped. I went with her and my daughter to the hospital and then to the same community crisis center where I had sought counseling years before. I tried to provide them as much support as possible, and I knew I was dealing with more emotions than usual, but I decided to go ahead with our planned trip. I didn't anticipate how deeply the events affected me; I was used to burying these intense emotions away. I had no idea how the mushrooms would peel back those internal walls.

We chewed up the dried mushrooms and quickly chased them with juice to hide the flavor. *(It's not so delicious, but what you would expect from eating a dried mushroom.)* At first, I didn't feel much of anything. I started yawning, and then I felt a little nauseous. My head started to spin, and I wanted to sit down. Les was renting a cabin in the forest at the time. We laid on a double hammock on the deck, looking at the trees, and talked all afternoon.

I didn't realize that what happened to my daughter's friend triggered all of my deep feelings of being unable to protect my kids. It all came flooding back. Inside of me was a vast glass wall holding all of my emotions back, and every day, these emotions were waves pounding against that glass. The thick glass held firm and kept it back, allowing me to cope and function. Suddenly, the medicine lowered that glass, and I felt viscerally the darkness I had been drowning in. I cried and cried.

My emotions hit my mind in colors. I felt deep despair and saw black. I experienced intense anger at all the years of being helpless to protect my kids and myself, so many nights of shaking in terror in our own home, which should have been the safest place in the world. I was angry about what happened with my daughter's friend. Every time I felt fury, I saw red washing across my mind. As Les talked to me and helped me process current and past events, I saw yellow as my heart felt warm and loved.

The forest around us was an intense green, and the canopy of trees above was moving and making fractal patterns. Birds were chirping from the branches of the pines, and squirrels were playing, running up and down the trees. I perceived such intense emotion that I had no idea how I could put myself back together and go back to work the following day. I felt extreme guilt for being a bummer to be with, not the life of the psychedelic party. I came face to face with that ocean of sadness inside and didn't know how to cope.

Laying in the sun and feeling the warmth on my skin helped me pull back from the overwhelming darkness I felt inside. His words and logic helped me navigate the waves as Les kept talking. Slowly, the emotion receded. I gradually felt the walls come back up internally. I was still acutely aware of the sadness inside me, but it felt manageable again. The trip lasted about 4 hours. By the end, I was emotionally exhausted.

Surprisingly, I never again felt such intense emotions about what happened that week. I processed everything that afternoon. As I continued to support my daughter and her friend in the coming weeks, I sensed sadness and other related emotions, but they weren't overwhelming anymore. To this day, I can look back and see incredible healing from that afternoon. It wasn't fun. It was overwhelming. It was months of therapy condensed into a few short hours. This trip was my first encounter with the emotions I had been burying inside for decades. A therapist once told me if I didn't process the feelings, they were going to come out sideways. I had tried, but what was still in there affected me most, and I had much more work to do.

After more research and working up the nerve, we set the date to do a heroic dose of mushrooms. This trip would be a first for both of us. I was hopeful this would cause a significant breakthrough in depression. We talked a lot about set and setting. I didn't want to feel afraid or paranoid. We didn't want anything from our setting to contribute to negative emotions or a bad experience. We both felt healing and peace in the forest and decided to be outside on a blanket, lying on the ground. As it was summer in the Western U.S., the monsoons were coming and going depending on the day, but we loved the rain and decided to take the chance outside.

It wasn't what I expected and counted as a "bad" or "challenging" trip, but it *was* life changing. I called in to work after the experience. The following is a journal entry I wrote that day, sitting in the forest so I could feel the earth and trees around me:

Dear God,

I stayed home today. I've been struggling to go to work at all. I think I need to figure out some balance. I feel so unmotivated. I want to move into my car for a while and rest. Be. Les and I did a heroic dose of mushrooms this weekend, and I guess I had a bad trip. I'm going to try to write down what I remember. However, the longer I am away from it, the more distant it becomes, and only impressions remain.

It started, and I lost my equilibrium. Everything felt off balance and like swimming through water when walking. I knew I would have to lie down when it kicked in, and I was hurrying to put away the food because it started raining, and we had to come inside. One of the first things I noticed was that I didn't care about things anymore and seemed unable to make decisions. Les asked if we should go inside, and I couldn't possibly choose and didn't care. I guess that was the prefrontal cortex going out. Then, the off-balance equilibrium. We went upstairs and lay down.

I wanted to be natural and close. I asked Les if he wanted to take our clothes off, and we did, cuddling naked in bed. The light started to hurt my eyes, so I pulled the covers up, but I also felt claustrophobic and like it was hard to breathe. I kept getting hot and had to throw the covers back, but I was sensitive to light and wanted to be in the dark. My mind was like a world by itself; every time I closed my eyes, it was like I went inside my mind. Throughout the trip, I could open my eyes and immediately reorient to where I was, and I didn't experience ego-death.

I was cuddling with Les and started to feel turned on. I vividly remember touching him very erect, and it felt amazing. He was touching me, and his fingers inside of me were ice cold, which was unusual because he always runs so hot, and I'm the cold one. I wanted him inside of me, so I moved to be closer, and then all of the desire just fell away.

I started feeling a lot of emotion. I cried about my grandmother dying off and on the whole time. When I closed my eyes, I saw black and some small colors, but nothing like watching a light show or something. I was trying not to cry or talk to Les too much because I felt like he had his trip going on, and I didn't want to mess it up. I'm disappointed in myself that I'm always crying and experiencing these intense emotions.

I guess I get worried I'm going to annoy him or ruin a trip he needs because I'm such a mess. I was trying to keep it all inside. I cried a lot. I guess part of me still feels like I need more of that – there is so much unhealed inside of me. I can understand how everything built up into an overwhelming mountain of pain and grief, a mountain that still threatens to fall on me.

I started thinking about my grandma, and I kept seeing her setting herself to die. She just made up her mind and stopped eating and died. I am in awe of that strength of will. She seems unstoppable. I feel an irreplaceable loss with her gone. There is no one else in my family I can talk to like her. I wish I could tell her about everything that has happened, the choices I've made, and the feelings I have.

I felt myself dissolving a bit. I was sinking into the bed. I didn't know where Les stopped and where I started; I sensed us together. I began to get afraid, and I asked him if we were going to die from this, and he said, "No" and "I've got you." I distinctly remember not being able to feel anything except his arm around me. I wonder if the trip would have been better if I could have talked to him more. I didn't want to bug him. I felt torn between trying to work on my healing and trying to help him heal. I kept going back and forth in my head.

I thought about my grandmother dying again, and I was wondering how she reached this point. She was ready to face whatever came after. I didn't feel much of my body; I knew Les was there. I wanted to let go and dive into the trip into my mind. It was frustrating because every time I opened my eyes, I was right back to reality, so I would close my eyes and go back into my mind.

As I thought about my grandmother dying, I had this overwhelming feeling I was going to Hell. I looked over this abyss in my mind, and I knew I was going to Hell. I fought it; I didn't want to experience Hell. I forced myself to think about light and love and pictured myself following Jesus. I was fighting inside my mind. Another part of myself was telling me, "Don't fight it; they say it is horrible if you fight it; just let go." I knew 100% that if I let go, I was going to Hell. The only thing stopping me from going into that abyss was my mind. I heard a thought, "You're not ready." I thought of my grandma again; how did she get to this place where she was ready and decided to die? I kept fighting to direct my thoughts upward. I asked myself why I believed in Heaven and Hell. I asked this over and over.

I kept sensing myself on a mountainside under trees, reaching down and touching the soil. When I was pulled away into my mind, I felt grounded by reaching down and touching the soil. It strangely matches my weird desire to lie down on the ground outside naked when I'm significantly depressed.

In that abyss was a feeling of sheer terror, and I felt that at my very core. Overwhelming mind-breaking terror. I asked again, "Why do I even believe all this?" I knew 100% that this life isn't all there is. I touched the earth and knew someone had created the world. My mind then asked, "Who is the Creator?" "Is He the God of the Bible, or do I just believe that because of how I was raised?" My mind answered that it didn't matter; there was no escaping these beliefs. My brain is formed and has accepted the Christian view of God, and I can't shake it.

My mind split into several directions of thought, and I kept trying to track them down. My brain was processing x1000, and I felt on the edge of finally figuring some things out. I kept jumping to all the areas that overwhelmed me: My kids, my failed marriages, work, demands from others, and what I believe. My brain was trying to follow all of these paths to figure it out, and it was too much. I knew I needed to focus on one area to nail it down, but my brain wanted to go to all the issues. It was like I could trace the neurons in my mind, and if I followed it back enough, I would find answers, but I couldn't get there.

Even as I felt it start to wear off, I was so frustrated and felt like I HAD to take more mushrooms no matter what because I needed answers. But I also felt terror.

I latched onto thoughts about [2nd ex-husband] and tried to trace back every memory and figure out what went wrong. I kept looking, asking what had happened. When I thought of him, I sensed so much rage. It scared me some. I could feel the hurt underneath. I remembered him saying how I broke his heart. I kept trying to figure out where we got off track. I was saying I'm sorry over and over. I kept trying to figure out what he wanted out of our relationship and what he wanted in life, and it kept coming up blank. I kept trying and trying to figure it out, and my brain kept getting pulled away. I couldn't get to the bottom of it. I think now that it's because I still don't know. I didn't know then and don't know now. Something huge was missing, and I don't know what it was.

My mind branched to my kids, and I felt overwhelmed. I felt so guilty for not giving them a good childhood and because I couldn't be there for them anymore. I had a strong sense I needed to help [my son] more than anyone else. I needed to tell them I love them but can't hang on much longer. I must warn them they need to find stability because I can't keep it together much longer or be the person they lean on.

I sensed this web of people all around me in my life, everyone wanting something. [My bosses] want me to be a strong manager, and everyone at work branching off. For my kids, though, it's almost like everything with them is SO DEEPLY hurtful. My brain shied away from diving too deep in that direction. I sensed my mom, dad, and brothers strongly and felt overwhelmed by what they wanted me to be and do. This web of people and expectations felt overwhelming, and I felt bone-deep, soul-deep, tired. I just can't anymore. I felt this fragile barrier holding it all together but knew it was limited. I felt the strong sense to warn everyone I couldn't hold on much longer.

Through it all, I kept screaming inside, "I'm sorry! I'm sorry!" like I was sorry for everything I had ever done. All I could see was failure. I was sorry for being. I was ashamed because I knew I couldn't keep going much longer and would let people down even more. I want to run and hide and be left alone. The stress is overwhelming, and my soul is tired.

I talked to Les for a little bit. I could sense so much hurt in him, which surprised me because it seemed equal to my own, and I always thought I was the damaged one. I thought about how he feels badness or darkness deep inside and keeps it locked away. It was like I could sense his essence; it was good, caring, and safe. I felt 100% secure with him. If I were powerless around him, he would be safe, and I could trust him. I wanted to convince him of what I could feel and know about him. I wanted to see him find healing. We talked briefly about his brother, his past, and why he feels he's a bad person. I felt such a dissonance between what he believed about himself and what I could sense so strongly.

Then, my mind jumped back to questions about God. It kept jumping from topic to topic, and I heard this question, "Do you want healing or want to figure it out?" It was like when I was in EMDR, and my brain jumped all over because there were so many places to heal, and I didn't even know where to start.

I was feeling overwhelmed and like a failure. I kept saying I was sorry but felt so so tired. I heard, "Why do you hate yourself so much?"

It was pouring rain and hailing outside. We were in a cloud and could only see a few trees. It was so pretty, and I sat up to look at it. The decision to trip inside was a good one.

My brain returned to "How do you know there is a God?" I again felt myself standing on a mountain, touching the soil and thinking it came from somewhere. There's a Creator. My mind asked, "What does He want? What does that mean for you?" I asked again if I believe in the Christian God and again realized no matter why I do, I do. I could sense 100% there is more out there. Then my mind said, "If there's a Christian God, what does that mean for you?" and I knew 100% I was going to Hell.

I asked if I could do anything to stop it. How was I sinning? The only thing I could see was sex outside of marriage. Even now, I don't think drugs or alcohol are sinning. The actions people take while on a substance could be sinful. I asked myself if I should marry Les to have peace about being with him. I know I'm already that committed to him. I already failed two marriages as a Christian; who am I to think a third can ever be okay? It doesn't matter what I do. I've failed, and I'm going to Hell when I die.

I thought again of my grandmother. How she was able to decide she was ready and face it. I saw my life stretching out as a temporary avoidance of the inevitable. Everything felt meaningless. The best choice was to gather my courage and determination and face Hell now. I truly believed the best course was to kill myself. I've already failed and am so tired of prolonging the inevitable. I kept saying I was sorry repeatedly, but there was no forgiveness for me. I was crying more and told Les. I had such a strong urge to kill myself right then.

He held me and asked me to wait a little longer. To die with mushrooms before dying for real. He asked for a little more time to figure it out. I really love him. I don't want to leave him alone because I know it would be life-ending for me if he left. So, I cried while he held me. We talked about it all a lot. I guess I have a few conclusions, but the worst part is feeling so terrified to die, knowing I'm going to Hell. I kept thinking how I used my mind not to go to Hell this time, and yet I know one day I won't have that, and all that will be left is my subconscious, and it is 100% convinced in Heaven, Hell, and the abyss for me.

The realization hit me that death would be a terrible thing for me because I would be fighting not to go to Hell, like on this trip. It made me want to face it and get it over with.

It's been three days. I still feel exhausted. I took today off. I feel bad, but I'm so close to just quitting altogether. I'm trying to hold on. I started using my FMLA for the first time. I don't know what I'm going to do. My motivation is just gone. I want to crawl in bed and never come out.

When I think I have to work to eat, I feel okay with some writing. But that's it. My soul is tired, and this trip emphasized it. It's like my mind solidified every nasty or negative belief. I'm a failure. I hate myself. God hates me. I'm not good enough. I'm going to Hell. There is no forgiveness for me. Even now, I know I can logically solve all of these. I have no idea how to fix my subconscious. I feel angry. Why was I raised like this? Why are we told we are either miserable in life or go to Hell? I want so much to sit down and talk to Jesus about all of it.

I do remember thinking I forgive- everyone. I am not holding on to negative emotions about [first ex] or [second ex] or anyone who has hurt me. I like that and am not surprised to find that in myself. What do I do to forgive and love myself? How do I get back any motivation for life? How do I fix this?

I feel okay when I'm off work and with Les. There are zero negative emotions associated with Les and our relationship. I don't know how to heal myself. I feel convinced there's a ticking clock for how long I can keep myself together. I hope to hold it together long enough to find a place to land and put myself back together.

In the meantime, Les and I are reading the words of Jesus. I love him. I appreciate him trying to help me figure this out. He said we could get married if I needed to. Then last night *he asked me. I know we are both committed inside to each other. I'm so grateful for him. I have never met someone who understands and compliments me as an ideal match. We see the best in each other and are crazy about each other, even with flaws. Thank you for him in my life.*

Love, Byrd

I was depressed for a week after this trip. Looking back, it brought everything under the surface to the forefront, and I faced it all during that one session. I gained tremendous insight into the areas I needed to work on healing. The mountain of emotions I was facing was brought to the forefront piece by piece, and in the years after, I spent time working through every single issue raised during this one experience.

Dosage and Effects

Psilocybin mushrooms, and all psychedelics, are medicines that require knowledge of the doses that typically correspond to specific effects of the substance. In the case of shrooms, we will be discussing doses of dried whole mushrooms. There is some variability in the amount of psilocybin in different strains of shrooms, but in general, dried shrooms contain about 1% psilocybin by weight. Since we are working with whole mushrooms, our measurements will be in grams and fractions of grams.

Dosing for psilocybin mushrooms ranges greatly and can be very individualized. Factors such as when you last ate or when you previously used mushrooms can have an impact on how you are affected by different doses. We would recommend fasting for several hours before taking shrooms so that you have a more predictable experience.

Routes of Administration: Oral

Onset: 10 to 30 minutes

Peak: 1 hour after self-administration, you will be at the peak. The peak will last around 1 hour, depending on your dose. Larger doses result in higher, longer peaks with longer duration.

Duration: 4 to 6 hours

These dosing guidelines are a starting point. You will need to explore to discern how you each respond to different doses.

Tip: Fasting for 4 to 6 hours before ingesting psilocybin mushrooms can significantly reduce nausea and "buzzy" uncomfortable parts of the body high. If you find the nausea or body high uncomfortable, try fasting.

Psilocybin Mushroom Dose Guide:

Note: This guide is for psilocybin consumed orally as dried mushrooms or edibles with the equivalent dose (in grams) listed.

Microdose (0.1 to 0.5 grams)

Microdosing is typically the dose you can take and still go about your day. At this dose, no one will know you are on shrooms. You may or may not feel something at these doses, but there are many reported benefits of microdosing shrooms. Explore and see for yourself.

Mood Effects: You might feel a subtle lift in your mood, like a good day when things seem a bit brighter. Creativity could get a little boost, and you might find focusing on tasks easier.

Visual and Sensory Effects: Nothing crazy here; everything looks normal at the lower end (0.1 to 0.4 grams), just like any other day. At 0.5 grams, or thereabouts, you might notice how bright and pretty the lights are or see enhanced green in the leaves of the trees on your hike.

Physical Body Effects: You're unlikely to feel any physical changes. It's super low-key.

Physical Activity: Go about your day as usual! Once you are comfortable with microdosing, you can work, play, and create on these lower doses.

Low-Dose (0.5 to 1.5 grams)

0.5 grams is where things start to get fun. Low-dose psilocybin mushrooms are very fun, social, and upbeat. We recommend low doses for activities like hiking, movies, concerts, etc. Be aware that things start to get "kinda funny," and you will not want to be at work, operating machinery, or doing something requiring coordination and total concentration.

Mood Effects: Things start to feel more upbeat. You might smile more, feel more open, and generally be in a better mood. Expect fits of giggles and laughter if socializing.

Visual and Sensory Effects: Colors may pop more, and things look sharper. It's like turning up the saturation on your TV. Your mood and senses will be a bit happier, and you will be more engaged with your surroundings.

Physical Body Effects: You may feel different at these doses. You will have a mild but noticeable body high at this dose. You might yawn and feel some "buzzing" sensations in your body as the effects become noticeable. At this dose and higher, the body high is more intrusive when you take mushrooms on a full stomach. Fast for 6+ hours before taking shrooms to mitigate some of the body high if that is bothersome to you.

Ability to be Physically Active: You can still move around pretty well but skip any activities requiring precise coordination. We love hiking with friends on low-dose psilocybin mushrooms. Outdoors is where you will want to be!

Moderate-Dose (2 to 3.5 grams)

As you move up to moderate doses of mushrooms, you will start to understand why shrooms are such a powerful psychedelic. Set and setting are going to be vital now. Be very mindful of your sessions at these doses. You may find that your experiences can range from very fun to reflective and healing.

Mood Effects: Things get deeper here. You might find yourself lost in thought, feeling connected to the moment, or just super happy and euphoric. You may also find yourself going inside and working on yourself. While many find happiness and euphoria, we have noticed that trips at this dose can be "darker" and dredge up negative emotions and experiences.

Visual and Sensory Effects: Now we're getting into the trippy zone. Patterns might dance around, and the world can seem alive in a new way. Music might feel extra awesome, too. You may think about things differently or make connections between experiences and thoughts that were previously impossible.

Physical Body Effects: Your body will feel different, and some nausea is possible. You might notice your heart beating faster. As with low doses, you will get some yawning and body buzzing as the trip starts. Moving around helps a lot to prevent the body high from feeling too intense.

Ability to be Physically Active: Coordination will be off, so it's probably not the best time to tackle a gnarly hike. You can move around but probably want to lie down and close your eyes as the trip peaks.

High Dose (3.5 to 5 grams)

Set, setting, and surrender: Don't do it if you don't have a safe place to trip. A bad set and setting can spin you off into a challenging trip. High-dose shroom trips are healing journeys, and you are allowing the plant medicine to show you what you need to grow and heal. This medicine may show you old memories, bring up past traumas, or allow you to process experiences differently. The trip will feel less in your control now; remember to surrender to the experience because you are here to heal. Remind yourself that psilocybin mushrooms are incredibly safe; you *will* be okay.

Mood Effects: This is intense. Emotions can go from super high to deep, happy to sad. It's possible to have very profound, even spiritual, experiences.

Visual and Sensory Effects: Reality can start to morph big time. With your eyes open, you may experience more halos, enhanced color/light, and some slight visuals (patterns, swirls, waves). Things change when you close your eyes, and you may experience another world.

Physical Body Effects: The body might feel weird with more intense nausea, dizziness, or a heavy feeling. That buzzing feeling in your body may be very intense at the onset of the experience. You may get the sensation of crawling out of your skin, but this should fade as the trip gets going.

Ability to be Physically Active: Moving around can be tricky. Best to stay in a safe, comfy spot.

Heroic Doses (5 grams and above)

Don't be a hero! Save this level of psychedelic experience for when you are more experienced and ready for a potentially life-changing experience. After taking a heroic dose, you may have a profoundly mystical/religious/spiritual trip. Set, setting, and surrender are essential to have the best experience possible, but the medicine may choose a more arduous path. Be prepared.

Mood Effects: This is the deep end of the pool. Emotions can be overwhelming, and experiences might feel life changing. It will be hard to predict what effects psilocybin will have on your mood since experiences at this level are highly individualized.

Visual and Sensory Effects: You're seeing the world differently and might even feel like you're in a completely new one. Hallucinations can be super intense. Some people find they have vivid hallucinations with their eyes open; others (us included) only have visual hallucinations with their eyes closed. Beyond your visual centers, you may have distorted perceptions of sounds, scents, and tastes.

Physical Body Effects: This can be rough on the body, with lots of nausea and maybe feeling disoriented. The body high may be very intense. We have found it very difficult to do anything but hunker down and ride out the trip. The body high you have experienced at the lower doses will be more pronounced at the Heroic and greater doses. Fasting for 4 to 6 hours before your trip can significantly reduce the negative body high.

Ability to be Physically Active: Moving around is the last thing on your mind now. It's best to chill in a safe, comfortable place where you don't have to do much. You should have eye covers or close the blinds because lights will feel extra bright, forcing you to close your eyes.

Risk, Safety, and Addiction:

Psilocybin mushrooms are safe. One way that researchers determine the safety of a drug or substance is to measure what the lethal dose is. We won't get into the details of this because it entails animal research, but the Mean (average) Lethal Dose is the amount of a substance that kills 50% of the rats. This measure is called the LD50, and everything has an LD50, even substances typically considered harmless, such as essential oils. The LD50 for psilocybin mushrooms in humans would be over 1 kilogram of dried mushrooms (or 1000 grams). For reference, a high dose of shrooms is 5-10 grams. So, we can call psilocybin mushrooms safe.

While shrooms pose very little threat to your body, your mind is another matter altogether. High doses of psilocybin can make you think you died. *(It's not as bad as it sounds)*. If you are naïve to psychedelics, I recommend starting slow and working your way up. Shrooms can be a light and gratifying experience at low doses, making nature more beautiful and music sound amazing.

What about bad trips? As with all psychedelics, you may find yourself scared and try to "control" the experience. Seeking control and fearing a lack of control will result in a "challenging experience," otherwise called a bad trip. Even in these circumstances, one can often learn something. A study released in 2022 found that 0.2% of 9233 magic mushroom users surveyed over a year experienced effects requiring emergent treatment. The most common complaints were psychological symptoms, including anxiety, panic, and paranoia. All but one of the participants returned to baseline within 24 hours, and the risk factors identified as contributing to these instances included poor set and setting and mixing substances. [55]

The best way to avoid a challenging experience is to remember you need to surrender to the medicine. Psychedelics force your mind to open and blend with your subconscious. If you fight this process, you will lose, and your experience will be challenging. By surrendering, even when scared, you will avoid this. Remind yourself you are safe, and the mushrooms can't kill you. Also, remember that your mind will return to normal. These two facts should be your mantra if you get scared as you delve into your consciousness.

For yet another win, psilocybin mushrooms are not addictive. If you take them too frequently, you will build up a tolerance and experience few effects, no matter how much you take. This tolerance builds in a day. For example, if you take 2 grams on Saturday and want to repeat that experience on Sunday, you will find that you barely feel the 2 grams. There is also no chemical hook, like in nicotine, to make you crave shrooms. So rest easy, psilocybin will not turn you into a shroom junkie.

Medication/Drug Interactions:

Cannabis- As with all psychedelics, cannabis has a strong and unpredictable synergy with psychedelics. As a force multiplier, remember that not only will the "positive" effects of the psychedelic be heightened. If combined, use much smaller doses of both substances and go slow.

Lithium- As a common psychiatric medication, Lithium can increase the risk of seizures and psychosis. Combining Lithium with any psychedelic is **strongly discouraged!** [41]

Tramadol- A prescription pain medication, it is known that Tramadol reduces the seizure threshold when combined with serotonergic drugs. (All psychedelics are considered serotonergic drugs.) Tramadol combined with shrooms also increases the risk for Serotonin Syndrome. [40]

Antidepressants (Selective Serotonin Reuptake Inhibitors)- SSRIs (e.g., Celexa, Prozac, Lexapro, Paxil) increase the body's systemic serotonin levels to treat depression. Psilocybin and all of the psychedelics in this book (excluding ketamine) are serotonergic, meaning they increase your levels of serotonin. When mixed with SSRIs, there is the potential for Serotonin Syndrome, a potentially life-threatening reaction. Serotonin Syndrome is not a common reaction, but it is possible. [42]

Les's Story

It is apt that we started with psilocybin mushrooms because that is where my journey with psychedelics took its first fledgling steps. Up to that point in my life, I had no experience with anything but cannabis and alcohol. I was always interested in psychedelics, but it seemed "too out of control" for me. Being "in control" was crucial to my psychological safety; my childhood and adult years were challenging.

Up to age 12, I would have thought I had a typical family. In some tragic way, I did. My father was often distant, impossible to please, and angry. He suffered from depression and drank alcohol excessively most of my life. I count myself thankful that he was not physically abusive, but that forced his frustrations into the emotional and psychological realm of abuse. My mother was a charismatic, argumentative, and imposing woman. She, too, suffered from periodic depression and was always searching for something, often adopting this or that faith for a moment. She also suffered from significant body image issues, chasing fad diets and fanatic exercise routines that spilled into every part of our lives. In those years up to age 12, she was my family's source of love and warmth.

From 12 to 13, my family life turned upside down. My distant, angry father had a psychological breakdown that would last a decade. My mother was diagnosed with Multiple Sclerosis and disappeared from our lives, only venturing forth occasionally. My brother Jimmy, five years younger than me, was the most affected by these changes. I was left to navigate "parenting" Jimmy, which was confusing and challenging for us. Our relationship was close and strained, as only siblings who have bonded through trauma can be.

I spent a good portion of this part of my childhood trying to keep my father and brother apart, as they were like fire and gasoline. Jimmy would vex my father like no one else, and my father would accuse my brother of being possessed or insist he had an alter-ego (which my dad named "Jake") that was the "bad" boy. The regular psychological abuse of my brother was hard to watch, and anytime I became involved, it would only make things worse for my brother and me.

While my father was impossible to deal with, I had learned to be sneaky and how to "manage" his anger so that it didn't get out of hand. Jimmy gave no fucks. He fought the oppression at every turn. There is one night I will never forget.

I don't recall our ages specifically, but I was about 15, and my brother was 10. Jimmy had done something against the rules, and my father was enraged. My mom and dad had finally given up and left us alone in the afternoon, retiring to their room to watch Fox News and smoke pot. At 7:00 or 8:00 p.m., my father came barreling into our aging single-wide living room, carrying his Bible. He began ranting about how Jimmy was demon-possessed and that he, my father, would exorcise that demon. With a violent monsoon storm, complete with apocalyptic crashes of thunder and lightning, crashing around our little trailer, my father began to shout scripture at Jimmy, calling the "demon" within him to "come out."

I don't remember how long it went on. The whole time, I was crying and shouting at my dad and then my mother when he wouldn't listen. I pleaded with him to stop as it was tearing my brother's soul apart. After too long, my mother pulled my dad back, saying, "That's enough." My mother dragged him back to their bedroom, where they stayed for the remainder of the night. My brother was a sobbing, fucked up mess. I was left to pick up the pieces and put my brother back together. Right before my brother passed, I brought up this memory, and he didn't remember it all. Only after I had shared many details did he start to recall it. He had wholly disassociated this, along with many other memories.

While that was the only exorcism in our home, the splitting of my brother's identity into Jimmy and "Jake" would continue, along with many more violations of my brother's psyche. As soon as I could drive, I spent less and less time at home. This distance continued as my relationship with my parents proceeded to deteriorate.

By the time I started college at age 20, I was trying to cut my parents off, but my family set the hooks very deep. Whether it was her illness or her natural predisposition, my mother became increasingly emotionally manipulative. Whenever I would pull away, she or my father would say how the stress of our relationship was causing her Multiple Sclerosis to "flare up." Through my time at university, I reduced my relationship with my parents to holidays and birthdays. I graduated from nursing school in 2012. While working out of state, I got a call I never expected and was horrified to hear my brother had committed suicide.

A month before, while back in my home state, I had run into my brother, and he told me the final chapter of his traumatic relationship with our parents. After I departed from the family, he became the "golden child." That is, until my parents, lost in their doomsday prepping conspiracy theory delusions, became paranoid that my brother would steal all of their guns and prepper stuff. At gunpoint, they kicked my brother out. He lived in his truck in the forest when he and I spoke. About a month later, after unsuccessfully seeking help for depression and anxiety from a local nurse practitioner (who accused him of seeking out narcotics), he took his life. I didn't even know he was that depressed, let alone that he had reached out for help only to be dismissed with his concerns unvalidated.

I laid his death at the feet of my parents, and that was the final straw. Right or wrong, that is my cross to bear. I still have work to do to forgive them fully. I stopped speaking to my parents that year and haven't regretted it. Over time, I reached the point where I no longer gave them any of my energy, good or bad. Sometimes, life requires explosives to dismantle dysfunctional systems, which would be a theme in my journey through life.

Let's fast forward through some traumatic years of a challenging marriage to a narcissist while raising two young girls and move on to where life found me experiencing a bit of a quarter-life crisis. It's 2018, and I have been working as an RN in mental health for six years. With the emerging research on psilocybin looking so promising, I decided to try it out myself. Lacking a street pharmacist or connected friend, and like the too-independent DIY'er I am, I ordered the necessary supplies and tended my little garden of mushrooms until they had grown tall and healthy.

I jumped in feet first and took 5 grams. The dose was supposed to be the "heroic" dose that would have you meeting God. Maybe that would have worked, but I was a bit of a sissy and didn't want to eat raw mushrooms. I had a brilliant idea and blended the shrooms into a smoothie. Right down the hatch! *(It was a big smoothie, too.)* This method of administration partially worked because the smoothie was tastier than any dried mushrooms I have eaten since.

I'll pause here. I had convinced the mother of my children to take the kids somewhere for the afternoon and locked *(yes, locked)* myself into my bedroom with the blackout shades shut tight. In the last chapter, we discussed set, setting, and surrender. *(I am sure you are seeing some issues already.)* I did not take these aspects of tripping very seriously the first time. I was more concerned about running naked through the neighborhood than fostering a safe environment to explore my consciousness.

That shroom smoothie digested slowly, resulting in a roller coaster high lasting several hours. The peaks had me fearing for my life and thinking Trey Anastasio (from Phish) was singing directly to me in a very creepy way. I felt trapped and at the mercy of Trey. You may ask, "Why Phish?" At the time, one of my good friends was a very experienced psychonaut and, more importantly for this story, a *huge* Phish fan. In college, he sold everything to purchase a Volvo wagon and follow the Phish tour for a couple of years. *(That's another level of Phish fan.)* This friend insisted that Phish was the only soundtrack one needed to experience the depths of psychedelics. Thus, on this fateful day, I was listening to Phish. I still don't know how Phish is supposed to assist in the use of psychedelics, and it may always remain a mystery to me. Learn from me and choose music that makes you and your partner happy. Psychonauts all have their favorite playlists, and they may share them with you, but I recommend picking your music.

For over 3 hours, I rode this wild high of ups and downs until it faded away, and I no longer felt trapped in my room. *(Still locked from the INSIDE.)* I had an incredible desire to go outside and see the trees and feel the sun. Finally free from my bedroom, I went outside to sit under the trees of my backyard with my fat Labrador, Huckleberry. I was calm and ecstatically happy. Despite the terror of the trip, everything around me was brighter and more colorful. Needing to be closer to people, I walked with Huckleberry. I smiled at everyone, talked to people experiencing homelessness, and felt supremely connected to the world. I'll never forget that feeling, and for a few weeks after, I was happy and noticed a decrease in anxiety and depression.

Despite the post-trip euphoria, I took four years to work up the courage to try another heroic dose. In the meantime, I grew more mushrooms and self-administered much smaller doses, both alone and with friends. I found 0.5 to 1 gram of shrooms could make a day at the pool sparkly and fun. I would take mushrooms a couple of times a month or not at all for several months. Nevertheless, I enjoyed micro-dosing very much. That first trip was a landmark moment in my life and, in hindsight, the first big step towards healing and becoming the man I am now.

Fast forward about three years, and my life underwent significant realignment. I was embroiled in a contentious and bitter divorce, trying to understand the actual toll of the emotional abuse I experienced over the past decades. I was struggling mightily, but I wasn't alone. Byrd and I found a deep and powerful love that stood like a strong tree in the gale force winds of life, protecting us from the thrashings of change we were both experiencing. Both Byrd and I were dealing with symptoms of depression and anxiety, though Byrd had much more. It broke my heart to see her mood so dark. With my limited experience, we embarked on a journey together to grow and use psilocybin mushrooms.

In hindsight, I am eternally grateful for our early success in growing mushrooms. Later, we would try to replicate our results and be disappointed to learn that growing mushrooms is more challenging than we thought. Our first growth yielded many mushrooms, and we were excited to try them out. My first experience with shrooms made me much more cautious this time around, and we started with a low dose *(about 0.5 grams)* and had a great time laughing and talking together.

While the first time taking shrooms together was upbeat and fun, I learned that mushrooms can have a profound healing effect, even at lower doses. During our second experience together, we each took around 2 grams of mushrooms. This dose was not a crazy high dose, and we expected to have a fun afternoon laying in the hammock together. That wasn't the case, and as shared earlier in this chapter, Byrd had a challenging yet healing trip.

While Byrd was processing her feelings and beginning to experience intense emotions, I felt euphoric and deeply connected as a couple and with the environment. My eyes were staring straight up through the ponderosa pines, taking in the wonder of nature. Byrd began to cry and withdraw into herself, and I realized I couldn't lose myself on the trip; my person needed me. Struggling not to become overawed, I slowly pulled Byrd out of her shell by asking what she was thinking. She began to talk about what she was sensing while I mostly listened.

This experience was profound for me as I was already feeling an extreme connection to Byrd, and now I was able to hold space for her while the medicine worked within her so strongly. I realized how honored I was to be with her while she was supremely vulnerable and fragile. I don't remember the whole afternoon, but I remember the feeling of "holding myself together" just enough to be a grounding, positive, and supportive partner. This experience wouldn't be the last time I maintained my grip on reality while tripping balls to hold space for my love.

Exploring psychedelics as a couple is an extension of your relationship in general. Psychedelics peel back the many layers we build over our soul and psyche, exposing our deepest fears, traumas, and insecurities. When exploring your consciousnesses together, you mustn't abandon your partner or judge them for how the medicine works within them. Sometimes, your intentions for a trip are to have fun and connect, but something challenging comes up for one of you. These are unique opportunities to support each other and "show up" like no one else can do.

Exploring psychedelics as a couple requires trust and safety. Some of these connections will stem from your relationship, and more will grow from challenging experiences when you hold space for each other. In the 2C-B Chapter, you will hear about an experience that grew our assurance and security in each other beyond what we thought possible. Even after two years of adventuring together, there was still a deeper level of reliance available to us, but it took a terrifying (for her) trip to attain.

After our 2 gram trip, we were more cautious. *(Unfortunately not careful enough.)* We decided we needed a heroic dose of mushrooms to attain the mystical experiences associated with healing. We chose to take 8 grams of mushrooms each. As the mushrooms began to hit, we fell into ourselves, holding each other but pulled into our minds. I remember feeling I had to hold onto Byrd as I drifted through the psychedelic landscape that bloomed behind my eyelids. Beyond knowing I had to hold onto her, I knew only my experience.

Things got very weird as the high intensified and I don't recall what transpired, only that I was carried along as I fell deeper and deeper. At one point, I realized I was only connected to my body by a fragile thread, and if I could go a little further, I would detach from the "self." I willed my psyche to break through that final barrier to ego death. And this is where things got strange and wondrous.

I went from drifting in space to seated in a forest glade. Towering pine trees swayed above me. Tufts of grass grew between the rocks and boulders embedded in this vibrant forest's dark, loamy soil. I was amazed as I looked around, feeling energy and life in the trees, grass, soil, and rocks. Everything had a life force in it. As I sensed my surroundings, I felt a life force blazing like the sun, infusing the world around me. Upon locating this energetic entity, I embarked on the journey of naming what I had found. Like any self-respecting human, I was intent on labeling this Being. After many adjectives and names, Earth Mother was the name that resonated with my soul.

What was the Earth Mother? She was my God, my spiritual guide to something larger than all of us. I was thrilled to be speaking to God. I asked Her what to do with my life—the wrong question. While the Earth Mother's energy was positive and loving, love is not always easy. With every wrong question, She showed me traumatic memory after traumatic memory and pulled forward the darkest moments of my childhood. I continued to ask questions but kept seeing the past, unhealed areas of my life. I did not find this process very helpful then, and it took me two years to fully understand this experience.

I don't recall my final moment with the Earth Mother anymore. I know it was a vision that resulted from a question I asked Her about Byrd. My vision panned away from the forest glade, and I realized a vast, lifeless desert surrounded me. In the distance, I saw a massive gray, upside-down tornado that disappeared into the sky and beyond. I knew this funnel cloud was the spirit and energy of the world's Christians, including my Byrd, communicating and connecting with the one God of the universe. My vision pulled back further as this vision and my time in the forest glade ended. I saw many energy funnels rising from many areas, reaching into space towards the God of us all. At that moment, I knew that we all commune with different faces of the same God, my guide being the Earth Mother.

I slipped back into the confusing expanse of the psychedelic trip as I slowly returned to myself. I have spent the years following this experience trying to understand what it all meant. It took another time in the forest glade of the Earth Mother *(two years later and thanks to ketamine)* and an Iboga trip to fully understand my first experience. As I asked the Earth Mother questions about the future, She showed me the deep wounds of my soul that I held onto.

At the time of my first and second Earth Mother encounters, I did not fully understand the wounds of my soul nor how I should heal them. It wouldn't be until my experience with Iboga that I fully accepted that I was already whole and healed. My "need to heal" was a self-imposed prison of my spirit. I thought the Earth Mother wanted me to seek healing for these wounds, but the lesson was that I am already whole. The traumas of my life are my wisdom and a gift to me and the world. I will speak more on this under Iboga, as there are still a lot of experiences to share before we meet Iboga.

Home Rolling

Let's focus on the set and setting of your adventures together—first, the dose matters. We highly recommend starting with low doses (0.5 to 2 grams). If you miss an element of the set or setting on low doses, the consequences are minor, but it can result in a very challenging experience at higher doses. Difficult experiences may be lessons you need, but if you don't do the work to understand and integrate a bad trip, you will have only the trauma of that experience. Face the challenges if they come up.

Low Doses

Set: Your mindset, mood, and energy for low-dose psilocybin adventure is not as important as it will be for large doses. However, if you are anxious or upset about something before the trip, you may find yourself carrying that mood into your trip. You need to be aware that psilocybin may not improve your mood and could end up feeling much more like therapy as opposed to a casual afternoon in nature.

Setting: You may not want to nestle in blankets in your comfy home space at lower doses. You may choose to sit in a park, go for a hike, or watch live entertainment. We love hiking with close friends or sitting together on a blanket in the forest when taking low doses of psilocybin. Have fun as you explore lower doses of shrooms, but remember, you will be intoxicated and unable to operate a vehicle for a few hours, so plan accordingly. Check the weather, have a plan for food and water, and bring everything you need to enjoy your trip together comfortably.

High Doses

Due to the intense and internalized trip induced by psilocybin, you may wish to alternate who takes a heroic dose. In reflection, we wish that the experience that was so challenging for Byrd was structured this way. It would have been helpful to talk through that experience as it happened and not after both of us had come down. Taking turns is not mandatory, but something to consider, particularly if one or both of you have significant histories of trauma.

Set: Be careful! Even in the best of moods, a heroic dose can drag you down a path that forces you to face hard truths or memories. High doses of psilocybin are medicine. You and your partner should take inventory of your moods, current life stressors, and energy levels before embarking on a high-dose trip.

Setting: As you explore more deeply with psilocybin, set, and setting will become vital to successful trips. Wherever you choose to trip, be sure you can stay there safely and uninterrupted for 4 to 6 plus hours. Your lifestyle will influence the "where." If you are most comfortable in your home, stay home when taking large doses of psilocybin. If you are an outdoorsy couple, you may want to hike into nature and find a secluded spot to trip.

Wherever you choose to trip, be sure you will be comfortable and safe. During the peak of your trip, it would be alarming to have a hiker stumble upon your secluded campsite or to hear the snuffling of an animal that elicits uncertainty or fear. For example, our area of the country does not have large populations of predators, which allows us to be more vulnerable outdoors without fearing a bear will devour us. If your home is like Grand

Central Station and people are coming and going unannounced, you may want to reserve your high-dose trips for times when you can stay in a hotel or rent a place for the weekend.

Set and setting are more complex as a couple, and you will need to negotiate your setting so that both of you feel safe and comfortable in your chosen space. When taking a self-assessment of your mood, mindset, and energy, you must also consider your partner's mood, mindset, and energy. If one of you is not in the right headspace to trip, don't do it. Consider rescheduling for another time, or maybe one of you can act as a trip sitter for the other. Initially, you may want to check in before starting each trip, no matter the substance. This way, you open up a safe space to discuss whether you are ready and able.

Use in Therapy

We have focused on how to get the most out of psilocybin mushrooms in the context of couples adventuring together to explore themselves and each other. We also described psilocybin as medicine, particularly when describing large doses. This description is not by mistake; high-dose psilocybin is being researched extensively for the treatment of depression and PTSD. Underground therapists use psilocybin to assist their clients in overcoming past traumas. *(Byrd's therapist offered to refer her to someone who integrates the use of psilocybin with therapy.)* Therapeutic doses used in research and by underground therapists tend to be in the heroic dose range, inducing a mystical experience that the researchers or therapists are assisting their patients in processing, understanding, and integrating. Therapists commonly used psilocybin before this medicine was made illegal as a result of the Controlled Substances Act in 1970. There is a rich and positive history of psilocybin use in therapy. While you may not see therapists overtly advertising this service currently, in the coming years, we will see the decriminalization of psilocybin for treatment.

Takeaways

Set and setting are essential, and a deep connection exists between mushrooms and nature.

Mushrooms are medicine. Very low doses can be fun, and hiking with 0.5 to 1 grams can make the forest come alive in a whole new way while allowing for extra fun and laughter with friends. Hiking on higher doses isn't recommended as your equilibrium becomes distorted.

A small dose 45 minutes before therapy can lower emotional defenses and make it easier to access the subconscious emotions inside.

Higher doses can be therapeutic, even if the trip is challenging. One must be ready to face what is inside.

Be very cautious about self-administering a high dose of mushrooms alone. Remember that a small percentage of people (0.2%) report psychological symptoms prompting contact with emergency services. Some describe feelings of happiness and euphoria with mushrooms. For Byrd, mushroom doses over 1 gram carry a sense of heaviness and darkness and access deep sadness. Even as time has gone by and Byrd's depression symptoms lessened, mushrooms brought Byrd back to the areas of regret and loss in life. [55]

Mushrooms vary in potency. We grew tiny mushrooms that packed a punch and giant mushrooms that didn't have as strong of an impact. Allow approximately 45 minutes after eating mushrooms for symptoms to begin. Wait about 60 minutes after the first dose before considering additional shrooms, allowing ample time for the medicine to take full effect. *(We have had friends experience unexpected adventures after taking more because the first dose took so long to kick in).*

Mushroom chocolate bars are enjoyable and tend to be more predictable with dosing.

Mushrooms make you hungry!!! Not at first, but after the trip, expect food to sound and taste amazing. *(Byrd may or may not have ordered half the menu at Sonic once after a mushroom trip!)*

MDMA: A Desert Trip Changed Our Lives (our favorite!)

Introduction

Methylenedioxymethamphetamine (MDMA), sometimes referred to as Ecstasy (pressed pills) or Molly/Mandy (pure crystals or powder), is a synthetic molecule that shares qualities with some classic psychedelics and stimulants but acts uniquely in the brain to induce sensations of deep connection, joy, and feelings of love. MDMA's chemical structure is similar to amphetamine, and while Molly is an analog of amphetamine, the structural differences in the molecule are the reason for MDMA's unique qualities. While it is chemically similar to speed, the effects, safety, and use of MDMA are entirely different.

MDMA triggers the release of several neurotransmitters, namely, serotonin, dopamine, and norepinephrine. Serotonin floods your brain, causing your mood to lift while reducing anxiety. Dopamine is a major contributor to your brain's reward system, causing a lift in mood and excitement. The stimulant effects of MDMA stem from the release of norepinephrine, increasing your energy and attention. Following these neurotransmitters, your endocrine system releases oxytocin, prolactin, and vasopressin. These molecules are what cause the connection, love, bonding, and trust enhancement found within the MDMA experience. [3] It is no wonder that people refer to MDMA as the love drug. The neurotransmitters and subsequent molecules released are similar to the body's natural responses to falling in love.

As our favorite substance, MDMA is something we feel should be shared widely, particularly among couples. Additionally, we have much experience to pull from as we make recommendations to you and others. If you search the internet and forums, you will find an overwhelming number of recommendations by very passionate MDMA consumers. I think it is important to mention that how we use MDMA is different from the masses of techno concertgoers, though I don't begrudge concertgoers for using MDMA in that way.

We have chosen only to use MDMA together while home rolling. We treat it as a sacred ritual in our relationship and seek to optimize the increased empathy, connection, and physicality of MDMA. Slightly different than our dosing advice for other substances, start low and slow; we typically suggest a medium dose for first-time couples. There are a couple of reasons for this, but our main reason is that your first time will be extraordinary, and you will likely never have a repeat of that first experience. For this reason, we usually propose couples start at a 200 milligram (mg) dose for the first time.

After your first few experiences, you can explore the many ways to dose MDMA, whether in a single dose or in a series of doses intended to build upon and extend the high. Medication taken after the initial dose is known as "redosing," we will often use this terminology.

If you explore redosing, which we recommend for experienced couples, remember that MDMA is less effective with each subsequent dose. For example, we may take 200 mg of MDMA initially, 100 mg after the peak, and 100 mg as the second dose fades, but that last dose will have zero effect. Trust us; you will be wasting good MDMA if you try to keep redosing. We have found that after a higher initial dose, you can take one more maintenance dose right after the first peak, and you will feel the effects of this second dose mildly, but anything further typically has no effect. In our experience, 400 mg per night/day is the max. There are other ways to boost, optimize, change, and enhance MDMA's effects. We will discuss those in the chapter on Candy Flipping, the term used for mixing psychedelics to create different experiences or to extend certain aspects of the trip.

History

First synthesized over 100 years ago, MDMA has a long history of use and experimentation, with the early pioneers of psychedelics synthesizing and using MDMA more than 50 years ago. Recognized instantly for its potential to help others, early adopters of MDMA began using it for therapy to treat relationship problems and trauma-related disorders. [3] It didn't take long for the U.S. Government to shine its prohibition lights on MDMA, banning it in 1985. The ban did not end the story for MDMA, and underground therapists continued to use MDMA in therapy. The perceived benefits of MDMA's use were not limited to mental health treatment, and MDMA made its way into the recreational space, fueling the era of raves and electronic dance music festivals. Matching the feelings that MDMA enhances, the dance community adopted the mantra of Peace, Love, Unity, and Respect, which continues to be the ethos of the Electronic Dance Music (EDM) community. [3]

The move into dance culture caused a backlash from conservative government officials, resulting in propaganda campaigns stating that MDMA will put holes in your brain and cause untold amounts of damage to the morality of our country. This propaganda was a biased scare tactic, not fact. Despite these efforts, countless people used MDMA to feel greater connection, love, and empathy with their friends, family, and community.

In the past 20 years, the Multidisciplinary Association for Psychedelic Studies (MAPS) invested heavily in proving the therapeutic benefits of MDMA and completed Phase 1 and 2 clinical trials with great success. They are in the final stages of Phase 3 human trials, with U.S. Food and Drug Administration (FDA) approval on the horizon (as of the writing of this book). MAPS's advocacy for MDMA and other psychedelics, notably as tools for therapy, has contributed to the renaissance MDMA and psychedelics are seeing today.

Legal Status

MDMA continues to be a Schedule 1 substance. There are no states in the U.S. that have legalized MDMA, and it is unlikely that the FDA approval of MAPS's MDMA treatment protocol will have a considerable impact on the legality of MDMA. So, for now, MDMA remains a very illegal substance.

Byrd's Story

MDMA is why we wrote this book; it was the most life-changing event I have ever experienced. A trusted friend invited a few of us to a concert and said she had Molly to bring. I couldn't go to the concert as I was running an ultramarathon the following day, but I asked to purchase two of the Molly to try with Les. *(Because why not?)* I had heard Molly enhanced touch, and some reported sex on Molly was indescribable, so what was *not* to like? We researched MDMA and were comfortable that the drug was self-limiting and didn't facilitate addiction as the neurotransmitters need time to reset after use, and repeated additional doses are ineffective.

A couple of weeks later, we drove out into the desert. We wanted to be somewhere warm enough for winter camping and ideal for stargazing. We waited until dark and took a point each. *(No, we didn't know how much that was; we had heard a point was a dose, so bottoms up!)* Word on the street was Molly makes lights look cool, so we started a fire and sat there talking and waiting to see what would happen. About 45 minutes after self-administering, the flames and stars looked slightly different, maybe a little brighter, but hard to tell. My head started swimming a bit. I stood up, and my equilibrium felt off, so we decided to lie down.

We had an air mattress in the back of the truck bed, open to the night sky above and the desert around. Initially, I felt some mild nausea. *(Note: Byrd feels nauseous with every substance. *rolling eyes*)* We crawled under the covers naked to cuddle, looking up at the stars, and... spent the whole night *talking*. *(What?)* We were shocked to discover that while MDMA does affect touch, and we spent time caressing and cuddling, we were even more motivated to talk and talk and talk. We started touching and kissing, which felt beautiful. We began to move closer toward intercourse; however, while the touch was incredible, neither of us sensed our bodies moving past a plateau of feeling magically good to climax or orgasm. We continued cuddling, kissing, and talking, and the talking never stopped. Our hearts and souls connected more than our bodies.

I felt an incredible urge to tell Les everything about myself while learning everything I could about him. I wanted to talk forever, knowing and being known. Until now, some topics were too heavy for me to talk about, and sometimes, I would spend 10 minutes just trying to get a single word out. Even with Les reassuring me, I couldn't speak if I thought what I had to say was controversial, could cause a fight, or might lead us to break up. I experienced such intense fight or flight responses I would leave the house at random times, even 3 a.m., and head to the nearest trail to run. Les, in turn, felt intense rejection when I couldn't talk and instead left to run. With MDMA, those panicked emotions I sensed around specific topics were gone. I knew what I felt about an issue or event, but the reaction was *gone*. My emotions had taken a step back, and I could speak from the heart. In return, I knew his heart was hearing me. Instead of being powerless to intense sensations of survival or fear of how he would react, I could look past the surface reactions and see what my heart wanted to say. I had indescribable empathy and could hear what he said without bracing myself for hurt or how my insides would react. We could discuss intensely controversial and hurtful topics and past experiences without emotional distress or hurt. It was the most stunning experience I have had to date. We talked until the sun started to come up and then fell asleep.

The next day, we lay in the back of the truck under the winter sun, and it felt wonderful. The winter desert was a beautiful state of warm but not hot. Feeling the sun on my bare skin always soothes my soul. For the first time in years, I felt okay. Truly okay. I didn't feel overwhelmed, and I didn't feel emotional pain. I was floating in a calm cloud and felt fully in the moment and at peace. I could see the problems and pressures I faced in life, but they weren't overwhelming. I could focus on one day at a time, confident it would all work out.

After resting and napping the whole day, we spent another night in the desert and drove home. We felt dehydrated and realized we didn't drink much the entire night. *(Oh, right, there was some nausea with all those good feelings)*. Our tongues had a weird feeling, dry with some bumps on the side. We were intensely connected. The whole way back, we shared our astonishment about MDMA. We wanted to share this with the world, convinced that if we could sit world leaders in a room and give everyone a healthy dose, we could achieve world peace.

In the following weeks, we realized MDMA rewired our brains regarding communication. I could remember how it felt to converse while on MDMA and consciously take a step back from the emotions of a conversation and approach complex exchanges from the heart instead of being defensive. The change solidified for me one day when I felt hurt about a text exchange, and instead of responding, I called my family member and shared how my heart felt. I spoke about how I understood the text, yet also remembered the other person's kindness and reminded myself I was likely not understanding their intentions fully. We ended up having a great conversation, and even over the phone, the connection was real. What once would have devolved into weeks of hurt feelings, avoidance, and second-guessing what the other person *actually* meant became an opportunity for empathy and understanding. I was floored by how my mind was processing emotion differently, allowing me to stop and ask myself what I felt and wanted to accomplish in an exchange rather than simply reacting, stuck in familiar verbal ruts.

There is a downside to MDMA, as I learned the hard way. After returning from camping on Monday, we returned to our separate homes. Being alone for the first time after such a connecting experience combined with the continuing symptoms of depression I experienced daily. Together, these emotions hit me with a tidal wave of despair, loneliness, and pain. Having felt truly alright for the first time in so long and then being hit with the returning feelings of depression was intensely overwhelming and highlighted the emotional pain. The rollercoaster was so disorienting and painful that I didn't think I could ever use MDMA again. It just wasn't worth it to destabilize myself. I experienced thoughts of suicide and despaired I would never be mentally healthy long term. I was highly frustrated knowing a chemical had affected my mind so strongly that all of the symptoms of depression resolved for a time. The experience confirmed it was truly neurotransmitters in my brain that were malfunctioning and causing feelings of depression. It validated the belief that I wasn't depressed because I was doing something wrong or wasn't trying hard enough. My brain wasn't working quite right. This demonstration of the effect of malfunctioning neurotransmitters brought comfort but also frustration. (Why? Why wouldn't my brain work right? Others go through things and feel okay, so why couldn't I?)

During my next appointment with my psychiatric Nurse Practitioner (NP), I told her about my experience with MDMA and how, for the first time in so long, I felt genuinely okay. (I am so grateful for an NP I can be candid with!) We looked into the chemical makeup of MDMA (strong emphasis on dopamine and norepinephrine). Next, we changed my antidepressant from an SSRI (selective serotonin reuptake inhibitor) to an SNRI (serotonin-norepinephrine reuptake inhibitor). Eventually, we changed my medication to an NDRI (norepinephrine-dopamine reuptake inhibitor), and this was by far the most effective medication for treating my depression.

After this emotional rebound, Les and I agreed we would only use MDMA if we had a stretch of several days together afterward. We promised to spend at least three days following each MDMA experience together to avoid precipitated emotional withdrawal after such an intense connection. This practice served us well, and I never experienced such a severe drop after MDMA again. I also continued EMDR, and while the process was painful and slow, one by one, we began to turn off the thought loops of despair and hopelessness I would get stuck in, trapped under waves of emotion.

Over time, we learned to expect a bit of an emotional rebound after using MDMA, such as feeling flat or oddly anxious at random moments during the following week.

Symptoms are dose-dependent, with a low dose (1 point) causing few or no effects and higher doses (3 points) causing more noticeable feelings. Once we realized what to expect, we could take a step back, acknowledge the feeling and the rationale, and then wait a few days. We found that drinking electrolytes before, during, and after helped with side effects like jaw clenching, brain fog, tightness in the shoulders, and dehydration.

Our experience with MDMA was so intense and incredible we asked my friend if we could buy more. It was challenging to come by, and each time we used MDMA, we knew it might be the last. We purchased a test kit so we could ensure we weren't taking anything dangerous, such as fentanyl. We found out that home rolling is the use of MDMA by couples at home as a method to connect deeply. Many people use MDMA for concerts and parties, enhancing stimuli and a feeling of connection within the crowd. On the other hand, home rolling is done by a couple (or sometimes small tight-knit groups) to facilitate communication and profound connection, allowing couples to set aside outside stressors, focus on each other, and work through issues. To this day, we have never used MDMA with anyone else, preferring to keep this experience when we are alone together.

The next time we used MDMA, we were on the beach in Mexico. It. Was. Epic. We drank a glass of wine while watching the sunset on a blanket in the sand. As the sun went down and the tide went out, we each took a point of MDMA. For the first time, I distinctly saw the Milky Way. The stars were indescribably beautiful and clear. Previously, I always avoided Mexico in the summer because the daytime was just too hot. Now, I found out those summer *nights* were perfect! We skinny-dipped in the ocean, a first for me. We talked until our flip-flops started floating, realized the tide had caught us, and moved further up the beach. All night, we connected deeply as the tide chased us up the coast. We laughed, giggled, worked through trauma, and laughed again until sunrise. We could be silly and childish again.

By the time we headed back home, we had developed a plan. We were writing nursing content for websites and wanted to increase that income while creating a way to host MDMA retreats and consulting for couples. We had to share what we found with others. More and more, we could see how couples were losing connection with each other and struggling to discuss complex topics without devolving into fighting. Partners were treading the same dysfunctional ruts repeatedly and causing further relationship trauma. We saw salvageable relationships growing distant as lovers with good hearts struggled to figure out how to fix it. Realizing how much healing and progress we had found, we wanted to share this miracle with others.

Yet another weekend, we went camping in the mountains in the forest. We found a dirt road and followed it for miles. We set up camp and took 3 points of MDMA each. We had developed a fasting process, withholding food at least 4 hours before administration to increase the chances of the effects starting simultaneously for both of us. Unfortunately, we underestimated the overriding physiological impact of stress. I was tense and a little overwhelmed by events during the week, but I figured it would ease with the improved setting. I could not change my set as quickly, and I didn't know how intensely my gastrointestinal (GI) system reacts to stress. My body didn't digest the MDMA *at all*. Les began experiencing the expected effects of MDMA and wanted to talk, but I felt *nothing*. Les's pupils dilated while my pupils were normal, and I had no physical symptoms.

I felt increasingly frustrated and disappointed, and my overwhelming fight-or-flight response kicked in. Les felt very hurt as I became more distressed. Feeling the irrepressible urge to run, I agreed to drive us back home so I could "flight" while also staying together. Both of us were very disappointed. I cried driving home, still feeling no effects. This acute reaction would not be the last time I experienced such an intense need to flight while under the influence of a psychedelic.

After we got home, we talked for a while, and I cried some more. I felt more calm and physically relaxed. Unexpectedly, several hours after administration, the MDMA kicked in for me. By this time, Les was feeling few effects, long past the peak. I gained insight into how powerfully my body reacts to stress, and we developed a plan for breathing and meditation exercises before administering MDMA when I'm feeling high levels of stress.

Thoughts from EMDR: July 2023

I was in a session and couldn't get past my emotional barriers to actually feel anything about the event we were trying to process. I just felt... nothing... even though it haunted me years later.

After a few attempts, my therapist told me to instead focus on the sensations I felt in my body that night (while continuing the bilateral stimulation). Within a minute, I felt emotions related to the memories so strongly that I started crying.

This reaction defies logic to me, but 100% confirmed what she has told me many times—my nervous system and subconscious remember and react even when I'm not fully aware of the why.

Dosing Guideline

Common Routes of Administration:

Recommended:

Oral (crystals in capsules)- Capsules of pure MDMA are ideal; you can test the contents and will not have to deal with the taste of MDMA.

Oral (crystals dissolved in water)- MDMA tastes horrible, but mixed with a bit of juice or flavored drink, you will be able to get it down. Effects can set in faster; otherwise, the trip is similar to other routes.

Rectally (crystals dissolved in water)- Yes, while an unusual route, the rectal administration of MDMA is highly regarded by some and is commonly called "boofing." We haven't tried this, so we cannot offer personal feedback.

Not Recommended:

Oral (pressed tablets)- **Never trust pressed tablets** as they are impossible to test and rarely *(read: NEVER)* are pure MDMA.

Intranasal (snorting)- I'm not saying you can't. Still, MDMA will BURN your sinuses like Satan himself and result in a different feeling experience, with much more of a stimulant, speedy feel, while lacking much of the sensual qualities we seek.

Dosage and Effects

Onset: 30 to 60 minutes (oral)

Peak: 75 to 120 minutes (oral)

Duration: 3 to 6 hours (oral)

Low Dose (50 to 100 mg):

I can't say we have much experience with 50 mg doses of MDMA. Our typical "low dose" is 100 mg. MDMA is known for the comedown and potential dip in mood in the days following a trip; however, at 100 mg, you will not feel so depleted in the aftermath.

Also, 100 mg is a dose that can fit neatly into an afternoon without worrying about a considerable comedown or being unable to sleep after 5 or 6 hours. We love this dose for a quick afternoon of connection that doesn't require a day of recovery.

Mood: You may experience increased sociability, empathy, happiness, and contentment. Your capacity for love will increase dramatically, bringing you and your partner closer. "Talkie" is our term for the MDMA trips that have us chatting for hours with no end of topics to discuss.

Visual/Sensory: You will experience some light sensitivity; remember your pupils are dilating, and everything you see, hear, and touch will be more enjoyable. The music starts to sound amazing. Lights are enhanced; if you stare up into the stars, they will seem brighter and more "twinkly."

Touch: Separate from audio/visual sensory changes, your partner's touch may be enhanced moderately. Think of that spot on your neck or thigh that, when touched, sends a zing of energy through your body. Imagine that your whole body reacts like this, *and* your sensitive spot is even more sensitive.

Physical Effects: Mild stimulation, increased heart rate, and nausea are common but will not likely be too noticeable at this dose. You may also find your temperature regulation is off *(thank you, serotonin)*, and you may sweat or feel chilled at different times. Be aware of the actual temperature of your environment, especially when warm/hot, and be sure to drink plenty of fluids. MDMA, as a mild stimulant, will make dancing, making love, and otherwise moving about very easy and fun.

Medium Dose (200 mg):

Now we are starting to have some fun. 200 mg is a great middle dose that lends itself to being re-dosed (100 mg) after the peak. 200 mg trips can be intense with a high peak, or less severe and longer than usual. This dose is also our favorite for couples to start with. 200 mg will give that overwhelming sense of connection and love with an intensity that makes memories.

Mood: Your mood will be more affected at this dose with an increased sense of joy, love, and connection. As a couple, you may be happier and more connected to each other than ever. Discussing complex topics will be easier as the medicine positively affects your emotions and increases empathy.

Visual/Sensory: You will experience enhanced sensory perception, with colors appearing brighter and more sparkly. Sounds may be improved, with music sounding more beautiful and resonating more with your soul.

Touch: Oh boy, touch feels amazing at this dose. You may find that touching your partner will feel just as superb as when your partner touches you. The enhanced touch sensations go both ways and at the peak, there's a good chance both of you will be feeling *very* frisky and sexual.

Physical Effects: You will feel increased energy and alertness. Your body temperature regulation is even more affected at this dose, and you may be alternately hot or cold throughout the trip. You will also have an increased heart rate and blood pressure, which you likely will not notice, but if you do, it is normal. Another intriguing effect on the body is a decreased sense of pain. Les has significant back pain at times, and during an MDMA trip, he will not be bothered by the pain, though sometimes, the next day, he will feel it. With the increased energy and desire to move, you can dance or make love for hours. Some couples have experienced the need to be up and moving, while others, including us, can lay in bed for hours. *(Though we tend to be active while in bed!)*

Strong Dose (300 mg):

300 mg is about as high as we go for a single dose. You will experience a very significant high, with a peak effect that will potentially overwhelm your senses and result in a night you will never forget. 300 mg is a high dose, so you should be prepared to hydrate before, during, and after the trip. Dehydration is the most significant risk with high doses of MDMA, so drink water with electrolytes before and after the trip.

Mood: You will be super happy, full of love, and intensely connected to your partner. Euphoria is something we hadn't experienced before MDMA, but you will be on Cloud 9 for hours. Take advantage of the "talkie" part of this experience to work through issues that may cloud your connection.

Visual/Sensory: You will experience enhanced lights and colors with the possibility of some minor visual disturbances toward the end of the trip. These disturbances may present slight skewing of proportions and some static-like patterns in shadows. Not to freak you out, but things might look funny towards the end.

Touch: Amazing. Touching and being touched will be awesome. Sex and sensual caressing are overwhelming but still *breathtaking*. MDMA relaxes body tissues. *(Girls! MDMA can decrease the gag reflex, which means deep-throating is a whole new world on*

MDMA! You can do things you never thought possible! Take a moment to surprise your partner with your newfound magic mouth abilities.)

Physical Effects: You will experience increased heart rate, body temperature, and jaw clenching. Temperature regulation will be even more impacted, with sweating very common. For penis-owners, you may have trouble having or maintaining erections, though this is not guaranteed. For all genders, reaching orgasm will be very challenging. The sex will feel incredible, but you may not be able to reach climax, which can last through the entire trip and for up to a couple of days after. *(Don't worry; you will feel incredible and connected; this is largely inconsequential.)* You will have energy to burn, and dancing or being physical will not tire you. Be mindful of dehydration, but otherwise, have a blast.

Health Risk, Safety, and Addiction

MDMA has been used prolifically over the past 40 years, with an estimated number of doses consumed numbering in the hundreds of millions. [3] Early propaganda highlighted the alleged neurotoxicity (causing damage to the brain) of MDMA, which was not factual but stemmed from research conducted on methamphetamine. This molecularly similar substance is known to cause neurotoxicity. MDMA does not have any known neurotoxic effects and is widely thought to be safe. The most significant risk to your health when using MDMA is dehydration. This risk is easily mitigated by starting your trip hydrated and using electrolytes to bolster your hydration and electrolyte levels.

Safely using MDMA is relatively easy due to its overall safety. Two factors can significantly impact your safety while using MDMA: dehydration and mixing with certain other drugs. The first factor, dehydration, is easy to prevent by starting your trip hydrated and hydrating during and after the trip with water/electrolyte mixes. Dehydration is commonly seen in concertgoers dancing for hours in the heat but can also impact you while home rolling if you are unprepared.

The second factor, mixing MDMA with dangerous drugs, is the leading contributor to MDMA deaths. Opioids (e.g., oxycodone, heroin, codeine, and morphine), benzodiazepines (e.g., Valium, Xanax, and Ativan), and amphetamines/stimulants (e.g., cocaine, methamphetamine, and Adderall) are the most dangerous drugs to mix with MDMA. These drugs are hazardous individually and have contributed to the deaths of MDMA users. We do not recommend the use of opioids, benzodiazepines, or stimulants unless taken under the direction of a physician. If you are prescribed any of these medications, consult your physician before using MDMA or refrain from taking them on the days you plan to use MDMA.

Like so many other psychedelics, MDMA is nonaddictive due to the rapid depletion of your serotonin and other neurotransmitters during use. Once your serotonin is depleted, you will no longer feel the effects of MDMA. The depletion of neurotransmitters happens fast, preventing you from using MDMA to stay up for days or to use it within a few days of the last trip. This self-limitation built into MDMA makes abuse very difficult. It takes 1-2 weeks for your serotonin to replenish to the point where you can fully experience MDMA again, and even with increased doses, you will find the results disappointing.

Medication/Drug Interactions:

We recommend you discuss any psychedelic use while on prescription medications with your physician or pharmacist.

Cannabis- As with all psychedelics, cannabis has a solid and unpredictable synergy with psychedelics. As a force multiplier, remember that not only will the "positive" effects of the psychedelic be heightened. If combined, use much smaller doses of both substances and go slow.

Lithium- As a common psychiatric medication, Lithium has been reported to increase the risk of seizures and psychosis. Combining Lithium with any psychedelic is **strongly discouraged**!

Amphetamines/Cocaine- All psychedelics become dangerous when mixed with amphetamines, cocaine, or both. These are addictive and can cause Serotonin Syndrome, a life-threatening condition. A study of Serotonin Syndrome cases associated with MDMA found that all 20 cases were the result of mixing MDMA with amphetamines, cocaine, or opioids. [42]

Antidepressants (SSRIs)- SSRIs (e.g., Celexa, Prozac, Lexapro, Paxil) are sometimes suspected to increase the risk for Serotonin Syndrome, a potentially life-threatening condition, but research shows that SSRIs are low risk for this complication. That said, there is frequent anecdotal reporting of antidepressants decreasing the felt effects of MDMA.

Tramadol- A prescription pain medication, it is known that Tramadol reduces the seizure threshold when combined with serotonergic drugs (e.g., all psychedelics) and also increases the risk for Serotonin Syndrome. [40]

Les's Story

Psilocybin was a significant factor in my journey to understand and heal myself; however, MDMA is what caused me to see psychedelics as something everyone should have access to. Our first experience with MDMA changed our relationship and our lives.

Byrd and I started our relationship during a very turbulent time of life (divorces, midlife crisis, financial hardships, career dissatisfaction). We had a crazy connection and deep friendship but struggled with traumas from previous relationships with lots of internal barriers and conditioned responses.

Neither of us had any experience with MDMA, so when the opportunity came up to obtain MDMA, we jumped at it. We performed some Google research and, with plans for an upcoming camping trip, decided to take the plunge. I didn't know what to expect, but that night changed the course of our relationship and our lives. We talked for hours under the stars, kissed, caressed each other, and stared into the vastness of the starscape.

We talked about our fears, dreams, past, and future. I heard Byrd share her worries and concerns without taking them personally or becoming defensive, and in turn, I shared my heart without any fear. Only truth, raw and straight, was shared between us. After that experience, we learned how to repeat that level of fearless communication, slowly developing the ability to lower our fears and barriers for vulnerable honesty.

How does MDMA change old arguments?

You might be asking, "How does this all work?" "How will I be able to tell my partner my deepest, darkest secrets and desires?" I'll show you with the following exercise.

First, think about a topic you and your partner argue or disagree about regularly that never seems to resolve (e.g., finances, family, sex, chores). These issues are "swept under the rug" because the arguments don't help; if anything, they hurt your relationship. Now, let's go back to the last big fight. Feel the disagreement, remember the emotions, the fear, and the frustrations. Remember your fear as the argument started. What caused it? Did you say something that always triggers a response, or vice versa? Can you feel the back and forth, hurt, and pain? If you have been having this argument for years, you can probably argue both sides in your head.

Let's try an exercise together: Imagine you are calm, full of love, and not feeling all of those hurts that well up before the argument even begins, like you *hadn't* fought this battle a hundred times. As the discussion starts, you believe that your partner will hear you entirely and that you are safe. You are compelled to share your thoughts and feelings, completely and openly, on this topic. You are entering this discussion with honesty, love, and curiosity. Now imagine that your partner doesn't react like they always have before, but instead, take in everything you just said *with* an understanding of your heart's intent for that statement. They love you and want to understand your point of view with the same honesty, love, and curiosity you entered this discussion with. They take what you have said, digest it, and respond thoughtfully instead of from past hurts or insecurity. Their responses to your statements are heartfelt and full of understanding of your feelings and perspective. Now, imagine again that you hear their response and understand their heart and intent. Your whole conversation is like this: you *genuinely hear* the other without reacting automatically. You can discuss and understand why your partner responds the way they do, and your partner also understands your heart and mind. Imagine again what kind of solutions and understanding could come from this kind of conversation.

That's a sliver of what MDMA does for your communication. Our arguments are, more often than not, a result of our trauma, insecurities, and fears dictating how we hear or say something. Our fears of abandonment or being emotionally hurt cause overwhelming internal reactions that cloud our minds and block our hearts from truly hearing the other person. MDMA cuts through the automatic, "out of our control" responses we often find in unresolved arguments. These new communication patterns are not limited to just when you are under the influence of the medicine. You will remember how to communicate from an empathetic place. More importantly, your brain will be rewired with the "better" way to communicate, replacing those old broken patterns. It sounds too good to be real, but trust me, it works.

Guys, you might be thinking that this will never work and that exposing this amount of your heart can't end well. Emotions are a scary thing. We often fear being revealed as our true selves. I spent the first 30+ years of my life thinking there was an evil within me that would someday hurt those I loved the most. I thought I was a psychopath because I had built such high walls around my soft heart. I also believed that being vulnerable would make people think less of me. That was all untrue. My heart was kind, and by sharing the vulnerable parts of myself, I could connect better with everyone around me. So, guys, don't be afraid of your emotions. You won't suddenly be watching romcoms and burning through tissues like some teenage girl. Emotions take time to get used to because society tells boys and men to suppress those emotions. Give yourself grace and feel the world around you. You won't regret it!

Back to Molly! I have learned that MDMA trips come in 2 varieties: Talky and touchy. On some special nights, it is a lot of both. There is nothing quite like making love while bearing your mind and soul to your partner, all at the same time. The talky variety of trips are lovely and bonding experiences. Byrd and I have learned how to communicate during these types of trips. But, the touchy kind of trip- wow! Your whole body becomes as sensitive as your dick, and your dick is so sensitive it almost (but not entirely) isn't bearable. We *love* the touchy trips.

Initially, during the touchy trips, I experienced some issues maintaining an erection. While frustrating, everything still felt amazing. The dysfunction was weird because I didn't experience erectile issues while sober, but on MDMA, I had "whiskey dick." About a year ago, I started testosterone replacement. I have had low testosterone since I was 25, but I never sought treatment because I already struggled enough in a sexless marriage, and more testosterone sounded like torture. But, after starting testosterone, I was able to stay hard throughout the trip. Worth it!

Guys, a quick public service announcement on testosterone replacement: Mainstream doctors will only treat you for low testosterone if your T is below 300 (sometimes 200). These guidelines are bullshit. The natural healthy range for a man's testosterone is between 750-1200. If you are feeling tired, run-down, low energy, experiencing sexual issues, *and* your testosterone is below 750, seek the help of a specialist. Ask around, and you'll determine which doctors treat symptoms, not numbers. You might have to pay out of pocket (insurance usually only covers testosterone if under 300), but it will make a world of difference.

Another takeaway from MDMA is that when you are making love, giving and receiving feel equally astonishing. I love oral sex, both giving and receiving, and MDMA makes oral, going both ways, fucking incredible. You will learn much about your lover's body with your heightened senses, and her reactions will be more pronounced. Pay attention; you will learn to play her like a Stradivarius or Les Les!

So, if your girl hands you this book and you are reading this... Just fucking do it! I guarantee you won't regret this. You will be a better man on the other side, and unlike other psychedelic medicines, you will have a blast the whole time!

Home Rolling

After reading our stories, I am sure you can understand why home rolling is our favorite way to use MDMA. That is not to say that you and your partner should only home roll, but we believe that the most significant benefit for couples is to use MDMA together and alone. There is still value in set and setting, but unlike classic psychedelics, your risk of a bad trip is low. That said, paying attention to your set and setting can enhance your experiences and set the scene for healing, connection, and fun.

Your set, or mindset, going into an MDMA trip is essential, and it is vital to enter into these encounters with love and respect in your heart. Like all psychedelics, only use them with your partner if they are safe, both psychologically and physically. The openness during MDMA could be used against you by the wrong person.

The setting of your MDMA trip should be wherever you and your partner are most comfortable. We have used MDMA while camping in the desert, lying on the beach at night, in hotels, and at home. Where you choose to do MDMA should be somewhere you are unlikely to be interrupted. Take an inventory of what is comfortable for each of you and find common ground when choosing your environment. The main point is that you want someplace you are comfortable being intoxicated.

Use in Therapy

MDMA's use in therapy has been widespread since the 1980s and continues in research and underground mental health treatment. As a couple, you may enjoy the enhanced physical and sexual effects of MDMA; however, in therapy, the focus is on dropping some of your defenses and allowing you to "step out of yourself" as you describe traumatic events or work through mental health concerns. MDMA can give you the space to talk about events that would otherwise trigger you without experiencing the typical intense emotional reactions. MDMA helps your brain dissect those experiences while reprogramming your response to them. MDMA is highly effective in treating PTSD as it allows participants to describe and analyze traumatic events while not being triggered. [56]

Psychedelic-assisted therapies are the future of psychiatry. MAPS has done extraordinary research on MDMA for PTSD, and their work will impact thousands of people who have PTSD. [57] As mental health professionals, we are both excited about the implications of MDMA and other psychedelics for the millions of people suffering from mental health disorders.

Takeaways

Nature!!! Nothing is as gorgeous as being outside, watching the stars, and experiencing a breathtaking sunrise. Home is easier to control the temperature and physical comforts, but nothing beats the unending beauty of being outdoors. The stars look so amazing with dilated pupils.

If you have a sensitive stomach or are concerned about nausea, take an anti-emetic 30 minutes before self-administering the MDMA.

We can take a point of MDMA in the afternoon, have fun for 4 hours, and go to bed at a decent time. If we want to be up *all night,* we take 1 point of MDA or 3 points of MDMA, and we plan to sleep once the sun comes up.

We make a point to set aside time each time we use MDMA to ask each other hard questions. "Is there anything you want to tell me?" "Is there anything I can do differently to improve our relationship?" We ask the hard-to-discuss heart questions that come up like, "I felt jealous about xxx; is there anything I should be worried about?" We set aside this time to talk about anything we have been hesitant to bring up. As we have made this a practice while using MDMA, we have been able to transfer this to our general relationship, and now we don't have to wait to discuss threatening topics. This mindset has become a routine part of us. We learned what it feels like to be closely connected and discussed anything that causes a disturbance in that connection instead of waiting. We realize it's better to talk about things, sometimes over and over, instead of hoping issues will disappear.

Early on, we agreed if our relationship was on the rocks, we would share an MDMA session before ever breaking up for good. Now, we know that's not a concern, but we use these experiences to reconnect and grow as a couple.

We review our calendars and set aside time for the two of us one weekend a month before making other plans. We go camping, head out of town, or tell everyone we are gone for the weekend and have a staycation. We guard this time together and only make other plans if we carve out the same amount of time the week before or after just for us. This method of scheduling our time has helped our relationship stay strong, grounded, and profoundly connected.

SPECIAL NOTE: PURPLE MOLLY

What they say about the purple Molly is true! We heard rumors purple Molly has a *much* stronger effect, optimally enhancing physical touch and intensifying sex. We didn't believe it and were skeptical about the higher prices charged for purple MDMA versus other colors of MDMA. Some researchers say it's a placebo effect, and scientifically, the chemicals in purple MDMA are the same as the chemicals in any other color of MDMA. We counter this with the fact *that something* is different since the colors in the resulting crystal are different, *and* the effects are usually more touchy. After trying purple MDMA a few times, we are sold on the purple Molly phenomenon, placebo or not! We will happily pay a little more for the purple MDMA, and many other couples we know feel the same.

Testimonial from Fabio and Mishra

(names have been changed for privacy reasons):

Fabio and Mishra are two young women in their twenties and have been together for almost three years. They found themselves fighting with more frequency, struggling to communicate effectively, and noticed an increase in alcohol consumption. Mishra is outgoing and emotionally effusive, easily able to share her point of view. On the other hand, Fabio is quiet and laid back and finds being forthright about her opinions and needs challenging. The two struggled to find balance in their relationship and often argued due to not understanding each other's needs and requests. The two women decided to take MDMA together to connect more deeply and hopefully work through some of their repeated conflicting issues.

Fabio and Mishra later shared how MDMA changed their relationship, "The best part was the connection and sharing a new experience with your partner. Our communication has never been better. MDMA lets you talk calmly and logically about what you try to avoid or fight about. It brought us closer, and we could understand each other more deeply. MDMA allowed us to talk about topics that were upsetting and remain levelheaded. We discussed things we hadn't even thought to talk about before."

Fabio and Mishra related they had tried MDMA as part of a group and together alone as a couple. They shared, "Using it in a big group can affect the whole vibe and trip. Being with only the person you are closest to ensures the trip is connecting for the two of you and yields the best results." The two described how they prefer to "start earlier in the night" to avoid changes to their sleep schedules and noted, "It can be beneficial to take medicine beforehand as we can get nauseous at the beginning of the trip." Fabio and Mishra further stated, "Even if you don't think you and your partner have significant problems, it is also just a great time to have with the person you love."

Testimonial from Stew and Ann:

Before trying MDMA, Stew and Ann were married for 26 years and reported sharing a great relationship with excellent communication skills and an intense, intimate sex life. Stew and Ann heard MDMA was a sexy and fun way to connect as a couple and reached out to Byrd and Les for a consultation session before moving forward.

Stew and Ann prepared for the experience by creating a safe place, gathering the items they may need to be comfortable, and setting intentions. Afterward, Stew took time to share about their adventure. He relates the best part of the event was "The deep relational connection as a couple. This experience opens the mind in a manner that cannot be achieved any other way, sexually and on an intimate feeling level. It allowed us to see beyond the ordinary and feel deeply a desire to connect, like a thirst. Wanting to explore unknown territories or being touched and touching the other person. It opens a box in the heart that allows a person to go to the highest level, to feel using all our senses and feelings."

Stew and Ann found the three days following the MDMA trip to be a period of integration as a couple. "Medicines are very different in Ann's system. She does not do other drugs. It took her several days to ground and get back to her body. It wasn't easy to be around people. You want to allow lots of time for talking and processing the experience in a love space."

Stew also related, "Sometimes we can be too involved with day-to-day life, and we put our connection with loving each other on the back-burner. Not that we don't have love and express love daily, but it is often included at the end of a list of items. This experience allowed us to put everything else aside and be perfectly in the moment with each other for an extended period. Ann accepted Stew's talking and stressed to him that it was okay. Reassurance on her part was different. Usually, Stew reassures Ann!"

As part of their MDMA session, Stew and Ann were able to talk about some sensitive sexual topics formerly impossible to address. Ann enjoys anal sex and is open about it. Stew related that he desires anal penetration on occasion but was fearful of what Ann would think about him. He found the taboos of societal norms and his fear of his partner's opinion led him to be unwilling to participate in anal sex with his partner. While using MDMA, the couple was able to discuss their fears and desires openly. Stew states, "Discussing anal sex while on MDMA completely removed the fear. We had an intense conversation, and Ann reassured me it was okay to enjoy." By removing this internal conflict, Stew found the limiting beliefs dissolved. His prior belief system disappeared for good and carried over into life following their MDMA experience.

Stew shared, "The deep connection achieved with this experience is hard even to describe. The intensity of the emotional and physical feelings is on a level many people may never achieve throughout their lifetime. It's like being in a different realm of the universe where two people can be so closely in tune, so lovingly intertwined, and involved with every word, touch, and expression that it feels like our souls have become one. I can't think of a better way to improve an already good relationship. The positive impact stays with you for weeks, months, or maybe forever."

Testimonial from Cosmo and Helen:

Cosmo and Helen were married 14 years before trying MDMA for the first time. Helen grew up in a cult and, as an adult, has struggled to process years of childhood trauma, even after over a decade of working as a mental health RN. Both were married once before their current relationship. The couple reported, "This was one of the most deeply visceral sharing experiences I've ever had, and I'm so lucky to have had it with the love of my life."

Helen shared that her biggest hurdle was surrendering, "I had no compass for surrender; I didn't know how. I kept telling myself to sit and surrender. Cosmo was able to do that, but I was not. I had no idea that fear was the most significant piece I had to work through." Helen struggled with the body sensations at first. She expressed, "I was sitting in bed when I started to feel a warm tingle all over my body, and I could feel my pulse rate going up, and my hands started to sweat. I was terrified because I AM a control freak, and I had none. I kept telling myself to surrender, but the fear got ahold of me, and I started saying, "I shouldn't have done this." My jaw was clenching hard, and I was shaking all over, trying to talk through a clenched jaw and chattering teeth. The first few hours were hard because Cosmo got scared for me, but he stayed calm and turned the experience into a safe space for me."

Helen continued, "[I saw] in. his eyes nothing but love and care. I told him how much I loved him and kept asking him to "Keep me safe." I told him I'd never been safe, surrounded by a vast family and cult members and church members; I was never safe; I was never good enough. He looked into my eyes and said, "I've got you. It's all good. Let go of the fear." I knew his truth. I wanted to crawl inside him and be totally safe. There was definitely a substantial erotic component. I wanted to kiss, lick, and bite, in a way...consume him. It all felt soooo good. I noted his erection, so I sucked it into my mouth and used his body to slow my breathing and calm down, like a pacifier! I felt like he could touch my heart with his penis. The whole experience, when I stopped being afraid, was so visceral and vibrant. It was the closest to an out-of-body, into another-body experience I've ever had."

Helen also shared, "Touching Cosmo was like an accessible paradise. He was mine, and I was his. We wrapped each other up in sweat, tears, and love. We made love just to be inside of each other. The orgasm did not happen; it didn't seem possible, but it didn't matter because we were inside each other, mind and body. That was orgasmic. Ultimately, we stayed in bed for 24 hours; we talked until we couldn't anymore. This MDMA session was a talkie AND touchy experience. Cosmo told me he felt like a second fiddle to my first husband, who would always be number one, and that I could never love him the same way, but I could see that he loves me the way I am. I didn't need to fear that rejection again; I knew it was his truth and could acknowledge it."

"After 24 hours," Helen related, "My body was sore, and my jaw hurt from clenching it so hard for the first few hours, but my mind and heart were SO enlightened. I knew we had an incredible loving experience that now belongs to us forever. I realized how much I had withheld from Cosmo, who would give me the world. I withheld total acceptance and love because of my fear and need to keep myself safe. I withheld sex until he made it clear that he needed and wanted it. The sex was good (outside of the terrible menopause years). Still, I rarely initiated it, and that made him feel unloved and unwanted while I was ensuring that he wanted me by waiting for him to initiate. I LOVE sex! It has been the one place where I can give up that control feature that overwhelms my life. Some of my sexual fantasies involve being dominated and given no choice because then the responsibility for what I do lies with someone else because, you know...."All that carnal activity will send you to hell in a handbasket!" To date, our sex has been pretty vanilla, but who knows, in the future, anything is possible!"

Helen continued, "I experienced such rejection in my first marriage as soon as I was no longer perfect. The man I would have died for called me a "Fat Sloppy Pig" while I was carrying his child, and he would not touch me. I have never been sloppy, but I couldn't see that. He killed something in my soul, so the cycle of being imperfect and unworthy continued, even having married outside the church. I was afraid of living through that loss again, so I walled it all up and, in doing so, withheld absolute love and commitment from Cosmo, who would die for me. I wouldn't have believed that, but I saw it clearly. I babbled about never being good enough, no matter how hard I worked, no matter how hard I tried, no matter how much I loved, perfection was always out of reach. The rapture was not an option for me because I am a divorced woman; irredeemable, the love of a good man was not an option for me because I was "too fat and sloppy." I heard all these things from those who "loved me the most" and said them because they wanted me to be happy. I just needed to change who I am: dumb myself down because men don't like educated women, come home, be a good girl, wait for marriage to a Godly man, and receive my ticket to heaven. Otherwise, I have "accepted being lower than any ole slut dog or sow," and eternal damnation was all I had left.

In the end, Helen expressed, "We are now more than 48 hours in and still basking in the glow of what we shared. I want to tell any couple who is struggling to think about this kind of therapy. To date, this has been one of the most valuable experiences of my life. I NOW believe one can touch another place outside of gut reality. Cosmo and I chose to lock the doors, close the curtains, and stay at home in bed because that was the safest environment for our first time. One night of MDMA has drawn Cosmo and me through a cloud of unspoken issues. We said it all and fixed it after almost 14 years together, but that time does not feel wasted; everything comes at the right time. Now was the right time.

Cosmo disclosed, "I have never been one to open up about such intimate experiences. I'll say what I can. I am beyond happy that this took Helen through a gate she has been terrorized by her whole life. However, it was damn scary to witness. I think the MDMA helped me be in a very Zen place – probably because I have invested A LOT of effort in that direction for the past 30 years. However, because of her background, Helen has shied away from anything "woo-woo." I think my strong trust in all that is love and light kept us safe enough to get through to the sheer beauty that awaited on the other side. I gave her my heart and body to use in any way she needed to find a place of peace and acceptance to have the experience we were looking for. Now, we need to throw a big welcome home party for the REAL and utterly amazing person I get to spend the rest of my days with."

Cosmo and Helen also related, "[MDMA] has changed our dynamic completely. We are free to touch, feel, and experience the joy of completely belonging to each other."

Cosmo and Helen were able to process some relationship challenges. Helen shared, "We were able to clarify why we have struggled with fighting over certain subjects. Neither of us realized that some of the things he says and does trigger that deep fear response, and I didn't know that my trigger was fear and not anger. I prided myself on never being afraid but was full of fear. I didn't realize that he had been trying to accept being second fiddle, [afraid] I couldn't love him like I loved my first husband."

In closing, Helen and Cosmo recommended to other couples, "Don't be afraid. Have lots of water available. Get naked—it's the only way. Keep some high-protein snacks readily available. The first 8 hours were gone before we even realized. I want to run out and let others know they can fix these petty issues."

———————————————

MDA: Like MDMA, but... Different

Introduction

Methylenedioxyamphetamine (MDA) is the lesser-known relative of MDMA and is very similar to MDMA with a slightly different profile of effects. MDA is often called Sally and sold as MDMA, so be sure to test your drugs. MDA faced prohibition a decade before MDMA and was not picked up as readily for use in therapy. There are very few research articles investigating MDA, leaving us with the social and cultural record of the recreational use of MDA.

MDA is more potent than MDMA by weight, with 100 mg of MDA feeling like 200 to 300 mg of MDMA. Also, MDA's effects will last longer than MDMA, with trips commonly lasting between 6 and 8 hours. Where MDMA has a distinct onset, single peak, and come down, MDA's effects will peak and wane, rising up and down as the trip progresses, first growing in intensity and then waning as the trip winds down. We found that MDA's comedown is gentler due to those slowly diminishing ups and downs.

The effects of MDA are very similar to MDMA, which is what allows dealers to sell it as MDMA. MDA has slightly less of the sensual and touchy symptoms and will give you a little more of the stimulant feel. Some reports on MDA's effects mention that it is more psychedelic than MDMA. A friend of ours, who has a low threshold for psychedelic visual hallucinations, has experienced visual hallucinations from MDA. While we have not experienced visuals on MDA, those described are not intrusive or scary. Similar to MDMA, it is self-limiting and not abusable like amphetamines since you will run out of neurotransmitters and won't feel subsequent doses until you have recovered.

Speaking of recovery, MDA does not cause a significant drop in mood in the days following a trip. However, taking a high dose of MDA may cause a drop since your neurotransmitters are depleted more with additional medicine.

Routes of Administration

We have only experimented with oral MDA via capsules. Like MDMA, you can ingest MDA several ways but we have never had a desire to try other routes. There are many trip reports and personal opinions on how to take MDA online. We recommend starting with oral capsules before trying more "advanced" routes.

History

Given the underwhelming number of articles, books, and research on MDA, the history of MDA is thin. We know MDA was developed at the turn of the 20th century and researched in the '40s and '50s for use as an antidepressant and appetite suppressant. This research turned into a couple of patents that did not result in approved medications. MDA's history of use predates that of MDMA, thought to become somewhat prevalent in the late 1960s as a cheap and readily available substance until its prohibition in the mid-1960s. It is widely reported that MDA was used by the CIA during the MKUltra experiments, using psychedelics and other substances to attempt to control the minds of participants. In one experiment, an American tennis player, Harold Blauer, was given 450 mg of MDA intravenously (not recommended), which resulted in his death. The history of MDA is conspicuously sparse, especially given its close relation to MDMA, which has been the focus of research for over 50 years.

Legal Status

MDA, like MDMA, is a Schedule 1 substance. Unlike MDMA, MDA has little hope of being rescheduled as there are no current efforts to find medicinal use for MDA. For the time being, we will only find MDA through the Dark Web or drug dealers.

Byrd's Story

A couple I grew up with agreed to sell us some MDMA. While hanging out and exchanging accounts of how MDMA had revolutionized our relationships for the better, the husband suggested we try MDA. We had never heard of MDA or the difference between MDA and MDMA. We weren't interested in anything but MDMA, yet we agreed to try it once.

The best way to describe the difference between MDMA and MDA is that MDA lasts longer (you can expect 8 hours) with a lower peak, and one MDA is comparable to 2 to 3 MDMA. MDA encourages more of the talky and emotionally connecting aspects, while MDMA lends itself to higher peaks of physical desire.

MDA has less of a comedown at the end of the trip and during the following week. For those affected by the dramatic emotional drop at the end of an MDMA trip, using MDA can cause more of a slow, steady decline. MDMA at higher doses causes more side effects, such as jaw clenching, as opposed to MDA or low doses of MDMA.

A point of MDA and MDMA cost the same, but MDA lasts longer. Thus, MDA can be more affordable. After several times of taking MDA, we went back to MDMA alone for a trip. We realized there was a distinct difference in some of the feelings associated with MDMA, particularly the intense desire for physical touch.

Some complain MDA has more of a stimulant effect. Others prefer the gentler, shorter effects of a single point of MDMA (expect 4 hours), whereas MDA typically lasts closer to 8 hours. We have heard stories of people told a substance is MDMA and it's MDA. We even heard of one person selling MDA, and when no one wanted to buy it, he started telling people it was MDMA so it would sell. *(Did we mention the importance of testing?)*

Dosage and Effects

When dealing with MDMA and MDA, I would recommend testing the drug with a reagent test to identify which substance you are dealing with. As we mentioned above, MDA is more potent than MDMA, and if you don't know what substance you are dosing, you could end up having a trip many times stronger than you expected.

Onset: 30 to 60 minutes (oral)

Peak: 2.5 to 4 hours (oral)

Duration: 6 to 8 hours (oral)

Low-Dose (up to 100 mg):

While 100 mg is not a low dose, this is where we start with MDA. Why? Well, why not? We enjoy the trip of MDA at 100 and 200 mg and like the high highs associated with these doses. Feel free to explore; some people enjoy MDA at lower doses, starting at around 50 mg. If you're sensitive to, or do not like, stimulant effects, definitely consider a lower dose.

Mood: You will be experiencing feelings of happiness, joy, and sensuality. You will feel more empathetic and sociable, often described as closeness, love, or connection with others. Mood effects are similar to 200 mg of MDMA.

Visual/Sensory: Sound and lights get brighter and more beautiful. Music will be a stunning addition to your trip, enhancing the overall experience. Also, at this dose, any hallucinogenic effects are usually mild but can include altered visual and auditory perceptions.

Touch: Touching and being touched is enhanced, rivaling MDMA at times. Touch seems to be just as intense as MDMA until you try MDMA again, and then you realize that MDA falls just a bit short. It's still impressive, though.

Physical Effects: MDA will cause some clenching of the jaw, similar to MDMA, and you might feel that internal urge to move. Expect increased heart rate, elevated blood pressure, sweating, loss of temperature control, and jaw clenching. Sexual effects of MDA are similar to MDMA, with temperamental erections and difficult-to-achieve orgasms. *(And yet, it still feels beyond incredible!)* MDA's stimulant effect is slightly more significant than MDMA, so you may need to move around due to the stimulant-like effects.

High-Dose (150 to 250 mg):

We enjoy the high-dose option for MDA. The 200 to 250 mg dose is an intense experience and can be overwhelming and even disorienting at times; it is worth it if you are into that kind of thing. Some people don't like to be super intoxicated, and this wouldn't be the dose for them. MDA at this level is an unbelievable journey for experienced psychonaut couples. This dose will have after-effects similar to high doses of MDMA, though the comedown from the peak is more gentle as the high ebbs and flows until you no longer feel it.

Mood: You will be experiencing even more feelings of happiness, becoming euphoric at the peaks. You will feel incredibly empathetic and sociable, often described as closeness, love, or connection with others. Mood effects are similar to 300+ mg of MDMA. The peak of a high dose of MDA is a great time to talk about any concerns or sensitive topics in your relationship. In particular, MDA lends itself to physical and "talkie" connecting.

Visual/Sensory: Sound and lights get even brighter and more beautiful. Music will be an astonishing addition to your trip, enhancing the overall experience. At this dose, any hallucinogenic effects might be more pronounced and can include altered visual and auditory perceptions, typically not disturbing in nature.

Touch: Touching and being touched is significantly enhanced. Sensual massages and sex will feel amazing. You may find yourself touching every inch of your partner or, in turn, enjoying delicious sensitivity in every part of your body.

Physical Effects: This dose will cause clenching of the jaw, similar to MDMA, and you might feel more of that internal "disturbance" to move. Expect increased heart rate, elevated blood pressure, sweating, and mild loss of temperature control. As for sexual side effects, expect even more temperamental erections and likely no orgasms. *(It may sound hard to believe, but you will feel so good this will be a minor aspect of the overall adventure.)* High-dose MDA may increase the speedy sensation, but you will not feel compelled to run a marathon. *(Though a desire to run into the surf to skinny dip at midnight might overcome you!)*

Health Risk, Safety, and Addiction

Little is known for sure about MDA. The research available is laughable and seems more consistent with newly synthesized substances. From what I could scrape from the bottom of the research paper dumpster, MDA has a similar risk profile as MDMA. That implies that MDA is relatively safe when consumed in the doses discussed here. [4] MDA won't be the first substance with little or no research present, but that doesn't mean I have to be happy about it.

We will assume that the limited research and the anecdotal evidence support MDA being as safe as MDMA. That said, two factors can significantly impact your safety while using MDA: dehydration and mixing MDA with certain other drugs. The first factor, dehydration, is easy to prevent by starting your trip hydrated and hydrating during and after the trip with water and electrolyte mixes. Dehydration is more common in concert-goers dancing for hours in the heat, but it can also impact those who are unprepared while home rolling since MDA will last up to 8 hours, compared to MDMA's 6 hours.

Assuming that MDA is similar to MDMA, mixing MDA with dangerous drugs could lead to severe consequences and death. Opioids (e.g., oxycodone, heroin, codeine, and morphine), benzodiazepines (e.g., Valium, Xanax, and Ativan), and amphetamines/stimulants (e.g., cocaine, methamphetamine, and Adderall) are drugs to avoid when using MDA. These drugs are dangerous individually and have contributed to the deaths of MDMA users. With the impact on MDA unknown, we will assume they pose a risk when mixed with MDA. We do not recommend the use of opioids, benzodiazepines, or stimulants unless taken under the direction of a physician. If prescribed these medications, you may want to refrain from taking MDA due to the unknown potential dangers associated with them.

I want to call our expert witnesses to the stand... us. In a combined 20 years of substance abuse treatment experience, we have never seen anyone addicted to MDA admitted for detox or rehab. There is no in-depth research on MDA, as it is often grouped with MDMA. Our experience professionally and personally leads us to believe that MDA is non-addictive for the same reasons as MDMA. After the depletion of your neurotransmitters, the drug becomes ineffective and requires a multi-day recovery period to recover. Regular and repeated use will result in tolerance and, eventually, the ineffectiveness of the substance. We can't say for sure, but MDA appears to pose the same risk as MDMA for addiction, which is essentially zero.

Medication/Drug Interactions:

We recommend you discuss any psychedelic use while on prescription medications with your physician or pharmacist.

Cannabis- As with all psychedelics, cannabis has a strong and unpredictable synergy with psychedelics. As a force multiplier, remember that not only will the "positive" effects of the psychedelic be heightened. If combined, use much smaller doses of both substances and go slow.

Lithium- As a common psychiatric medication, Lithium has been reported to increase the risk of seizures and psychosis. Combining Lithium with any psychedelic is **strongly discouraged!**

Amphetamines/Cocaine- All psychedelics become dangerous when mixed with amphetamines and cocaine. These are addictive and can cause Serotonin Syndrome, a life-threatening condition.

Antidepressants (SSRIs)- SSRIs (e.g., Celexa, Prozac, Lexapro, Paxil) are suspected to increase the risk for Serotonin Syndrome, a potentially life-threatening condition. Still, research shows that SSRIs are low risk for this complication. Of note, a study of Serotonin

Syndrome cases associated with MDMA found that all 20 cases were the result of mixing MDMA with amphetamines, cocaine, or opioids. [42] Last, there is frequent anecdotal reporting of antidepressants decreasing the felt effects of MDMA.

Tramadol- A prescription pain medication, it is known that Tramadol reduces the seizure threshold when combined with serotonergic drugs (e.g., all psychedelics) and also increases the risk for Serotonin Syndrome. [40]

Les's Story

MDA is so similar to MDMA that it takes a bit of experience with both to appreciate the differences fully. As Byrd said, MDA has more of the talkie effects, though it can, and will, enhance touch and sex similar to MDMA, but just a degree less. I love the length of the trip that comes from MDA.

My favorite MDA memory happened in 2022 when we got lucky with the weather. It was a dry year in the western U.S., and we spent the winter camping in the desert and the summer camping in the forests. July is monsoon season, and we had been avidly watching the weather for a break in the storms so we could go camping. Finally, the thunderstorms dried out, with only a chance of intermittent cloud cover and showers for most of the night. We longed to see the summer night sky and decided to risk the rain. So, we packed the truck and headed up into the mountains.

Buried in the mountain forest is a breathtaking, 200-mile-long rock shelf, popular as a camping and UTV recreation area. The area is tranquil when the weather rolls in. We crept the truck to the very edge of the lookout, with a 180-degree view of the valley below. It was breathtaking. Our "setting" was epic.

We took our MDA as the sun was setting over the hills of the small town below and settled into the truck bed, surrounded by tall ponderosa pines, with a verdant green valley of pines spread out below us. The trip was talkie and deeply connecting. Throughout the night, the clouds would obscure the sky and alternately reveal the near-full moon in its brilliance. Just the full moon over the drop-off was breathtaking.

The fantastic part of the night was how the wind was driving the clouds down in the valley up and over the 1000-foot higher rocky shelf. We watched the clouds fill the valley below and talked and laughed the night away, knowing the rain might start at any moment. As we lay in the pickup, riding the waves of MDA, the misty clouds flowed around us, creating this foggy, ephemeral fantasy landscape. Around 1 a.m., the air around us became unnaturally still, and clouds began rolling up over the cliff en masse, filling the forest around us. Soon, we were resting in a cloud, with zero visibility around us, tiny drops of water collecting and misting our sleeping bag. It was utterly magical.

For hours, the clouds rolled up and down the cliffside, first surrounding us, then thinning, and then thickening again. The forest was peaceful and quiet, just the two of us in the world. Byrd became tearful at the sheer beauty of the world, wishing we could stop time and hold the moment and each other forever. We were awed by the beauty of the clouds and fog all night. We have attempted, unsuccessfully, to recreate this setting many times.

Home Rolling

MDA is a fun and unique variant of MDMA that provides a slightly different flavor of experience while still retaining most of the loving, bonding, and sexy nature of MDMA. We treat MDA like MDMA when home rolling. Choose a private, comfy place that will leave you undisturbed for 6 to 8 hours. Bring some water, electrolytes, and snacks (if away from home) to support your bodies and brains during the trip.

Use in Therapy

MDA does not have a pedigreed history of therapeutic use like MDMA. In our research for this book, we found some individual accounts of therapists and psychedelic guides using MDA in the same way others use MDMA. It is happening out there, but the research and psychedelic community have not substantially incorporated MDA. From our experience, Sally is just as empathetic as MDMA, and we have found it great for connecting and having fun.

LSD: Couples That Trip Together Stay Together

Introduction

LSD, short for lysergic acid diethylamide, is a potent psychedelic that goes by many names: acid, blotter, tabs, and many more. LSD is very potent, with the doses measured in micrograms (ug or mcg) versus milligrams (mg). For this reason, acid is typically diluted in liquid form or infused into paper blotters. Blotter paper is the iconic form of acid. It is a sheet of thick paper, usually with a fun image printed on it, that is perforated to create tiny (¼ inch) squares. Each of these squares will be a single dose of acid, with doses ranging from 25 micrograms to over 300 micrograms, so be careful, as each square is not a standard dose. As such, a palm-sized sheet can have over two hundred doses of LSD.

Acid was initially daunting for us. We were raised on stories about LSD causing hallucinations and near insanity, instantly porting users to an alternate dimension full of frightening entities. Instead, we found a drug that is very predictable at different doses and can be extremely light and happy at low doses. LSD, under 300 ug, taken alone is a blast when kicking back with close friends, attending funerals, or visiting inmates in prison. It is also our favorite substance for raves because acid makes music sound like the angels are signing. On acid with the right crowd, you will get that sense of oneness, where you feel connected to everyone around you, and your hearts beat as one.

Before we continue, we would be remiss in mentioning another incredible characteristic of LSD. This substance has an excellent synergistic effect when mixed with other psychedelics. We will cover this information in the chapter on Candy Flipping but know that lower doses of LSD can extend, change, and enhance the effects of substances like MDMA or MDA.

History

In 1938, Swiss chemist Albert Hofmann quietly discovered LSD, but Hofmann wouldn't realize its psychoactive properties for another five years. LSD is derived from a fungus, ergot, that grows on grains and has an exciting history of causing individuals and whole towns to go "crazy" after consuming infected grains. On April 19, 1943, Hofmann ingested 250 micrograms of LSD and rode his bicycle home from his lab, embarking on a magical trip that inspired generations of psychonauts. Bicycle Day, celebrated around the world, is in honor of Hofmann's first intentional LSD trip. In 2018, the United Nations adopted Bicycle Day as a global holiday.

Fast forward to the beginning of the Cold War, and we find global powers on the verge of nuclear annihilation. The government superpowers explored the use of LSD for a multitude of military applications, including creating weapons that incapacitate the minds of the enemy without turning cities into plates of glass. LSD, among many other chemicals, was tested on soldiers and volunteers to determine whether psychoactive chemicals are weaponizable. The CIA, not be outdone, tested LSD in the illegal MKUltra program as a chemical agent to brainwash and make individuals more susceptible to coercion. [8] I find this horrifying, but if you are interested, the book *Chemical Warfare Secrets Almost Forgotten* details the experiments of that era. James Ketchum, one of the psychiatrists who worked in the program, wrote this account.

Research moved into the universities in the early 1960s. In a now-famous move, Timothy Leary and Richard Alpert at Harvard University distributed LSD widely in pseudo-research with the intent of expanding the consciousness of all. Leary coined the "Turn on, Tune in, and Drop Out" rally cry of the youth during the 1960s psychedelic movement. As expected, Leary and Alpert were fired from Harvard, but their work was already done, with LSD spreading like wildfire across the United States. [8]

In the United States, LSD quickly became illegal to quash the anti-Vietnam War cultural movement that was primarily composed of hippies using LSD. As with most of the drugs described in this book, LSD culture suffered from the War on Drugs, sending many people to jail for their participation in the cultural efforts to expand consciousness through LSD and other psychedelics.

We were saddened to read about the history of LSD and LSD Prisoners of War (POWs). For example, Timothy Leonard Tyler was sentenced to life in prison for possession and distribution of LSD at the age of 25. [22] He served 24 years and 27 days in prison until President Obama approved his pardon, releasing him on August 30, 2018. [23] Over 423,000 people signed the petition for his release. [24] Another LSD POW, Robert Riley, served over 23 years in prison for charges related to LSD and mushrooms until President Obama pardoned him on January 19, 2017. [25,26,27]

Leonard Pickard and Clyde Apperson are two more LSD POWs arrested in 2000 on charges related to creating and selling LSD. [28] Pickard was an honor student and named "most intellectual" in school. Pickard earned a scholarship to Princeton University, dropped out after one term, and functioned as the Drug Policy Research Program Deputy Director at the University of California, Los Angeles, until 1974. After the War on drugs began, he worked with partners, including Apperson, to covertly make and distribute LSD. After his arrest, he spent 17 years in prison in Arizona, writing a book, "The Rose of Paracelsus." Pickard was released on July 27, 2020, due to reasons of advanced age, medical conditions, and the COVID-19 epidemic. Apperson was released during the same time. [29]

As we listened, read, and watched documentaries, books, and podcasts about the history of LSD, we were struck by the pattern of those who experience LSD arriving at similar conclusions. Love is the answer. Let's seek peace in our world. Be kind. Let's change our world for the better. No more war. Whatever happens when people use LSD, the conclusions one reaches are very similar.

The criminalization of LSD halted most research into its therapeutic uses and stymied the therapists who were using LSD in psychotherapy. But, despite the illegality of LSD, thousands continued to use and share LSD. Today, with the psychedelic renaissance in full swing, we are seeing a resurgence of mainstream interest in LSD, opening the doors to research and therapeutic use. While psilocybin and MDMA have taken the top spots in research and advocacy, LSD is a highly therapeutic medicine that has similar implications in the treatment of psychological conditions.

Legal Status

You have probably already guessed, but LSD is very illegal. LSD is a Schedule I substance in the United States and looks to remain that way for some time to come. While psilocybin is seeing some progressive legislation at the state level, LSD has not been afforded the same consideration. It is unlikely we will see any rescheduling or decriminalization of LSD for many years to come.

Byrd's Story

When Les learned how to order substances on the Dark Web, we found LSD and wanted to try it. Les read research on the benefits of microdosing LSD and the related antidepressant benefits. After my experiences with mushrooms, I was nervous and wanted to start slow and ease myself into it.

LSD comes in paper squares, liquid drops, and gel tabs, measured in *micrograms,* not milligrams. We started with the paper tabs because we could cut these into smaller doses. The first time, we took ¼ of a tiny little paper tab (25 mcg), placing the paper between the tongue and gums to allow for absorption across the mucous membranes. I didn't even feel it. The second time, we did ½ of a paper tab (50 mcg) and went to a funeral. As the funeral was for someone I grew up with in the church I used to attend, there was some subconscious bracing myself for the experience. *(To be honest, this friend would have found it funny and not disrespectful or antagonistic.)* We felt the effects very mildly. I was a little floaty, but nothing that affected equilibrium. I was more relaxed and a little lighter and giggly. I was relieved the service didn't bring up a lot of negative emotions. We could easily walk around, talk, meet new people, and have a fun afternoon. I was ready to try more.

We went out to lunch with a friend and decided to take a full paper tab each (100 mcg) afterward. We drove out to the forest and lay in the dappled shade on a double hammock, talking and laughing. It was one of those perfect days in the forest, not too hot or cold, with a gentle breeze whistling through the pines. We found a secluded spot and, after making love, lay naked in the sun. My soul felt young, carefree, and warm. As the sun began to set, we drove back home.

On the way home, places I had driven past hundreds of times since childhood captured my attention. My brain processed everything around me like I had never seen, heard, or experienced these stimuli. I was seeing things for the first time, though I had seen them a hundred times before.

Music! The music was extraordinary beyond words. My ears and mind had never really heard music until now. My whole self was listening, sitting in the truck on the side of the road, enraptured with the sounds of the radio. We danced and laughed, picking out song after song. I had never experienced music like this before. *(The angels were singing pop music!)* To this day, LSD enhances music like no other substance I have ever tried.

We learned that LSD effects last for 12 hours. It takes roughly an hour to kick in after administration; the peak is 3 to 4 hours, and then there's a feeling of being lightly happy and very awake for another 8 hours. There is no withdrawal or comedown. The feelings slowly fade, leaving one very alert but oddly unfatigued for hours. We slept little that night and, the next day, felt refreshed as if we had slept twice as long. The contrast between the day after LSD and the feeling of waking up after having drunk too much alcohol the night before was stark. No hangover or heaviness. No emotional drop. LSD is immaculate energy. My mind felt refreshed, perceiving the world in a whole new way.

Whereas mushrooms have a dark and heavy feeling, LSD is light and happy. Both medicines allow for enhanced introspection and a new depth of perception. My stomach may become nauseous or cramp at doses higher than 200 mcg. I learned to self-administer an antiemetic or nausea medication before or at the same time as administering LSD to ease the effects on my stomach. I have a high concentration of serotonin receptors in my stomach, and different substances can affect my GI system.

I feel emotions in my stomach. Negative emotions, distress, and unhappiness all result in intense feelings of cramping and pain. When I'm sad, I don't eat. About six months after starting depression medication, I began gaining unexplained weight. After a period of gaining 2 pounds a week, I abruptly stopped my medication. *(Negative five stars - do not recommend this action!).* My psychiatric NP started a different medication and referred me to a GI specialist and then an endocrinologist. In the end, I was diagnosed with Barrett's esophagus and Hashimoto's. The areas in my stomach where I felt negative emotions the most were extensively damaged. Every spot biopsied for tissue damage brought back physically painful feelings of deep emotional distress during the most challenging moments of my life. To put it in perspective, people are often diagnosed with Barrett's esophagus after years of drinking heavily. In my case, I had only had occasional alcoholic drinks for one year of my life when I was diagnosed. Instead, the damage was due to intense stress. I was relieved to learn the cause of the weight gain and other symptoms but sad to see the effects of stress on my body.

We went to visit one of my brothers and tried 200 mcg of LSD together. We all spent the afternoon laughing, exchanging jokes, and trying to play Scrabble. Another time, we had a bonfire with friends, laughing and talking about deeply personal experiences for hours into the night. LSD at lower doses is very social, generating endless conversations about various topics. We went to a music festival and took 200 mcg of LSD. The experience was incredible, with beautiful music, lights, and connection. I was awestruck being together with thousands of others, happily listening to music, dancing, and loving life. I wondered why our world can't have more music festivals of love, peace, and goodwill. Why do we have to have all of the ugly things? Why do we continue traditions of pain like War and generational trauma? *(Oh no! I'm turning into a hippie!)*

One day, I decided to try a small dose of LSD while running an ultra-marathon. I had heard of an ultra-runner who won the 250-mile Cocodona Ultramarathon while microdosing on mushrooms. Substances like mushrooms make everything outdoors seem brighter and the forest more beautiful and sparkly, so why not? LSD lasts 12 hours, and I figured that was less than the time it would take to run the 55-kilometer race I had entered. Going with the micro-dosing idea, I self-administered 100 mcg at the start of the race. It was winter, so I figured any serotonin heat flushes wouldn't affect me much with the cool weather.

The race started the same as usual. I enjoy running and how ultra-marathons simplify life down to survival. Fuel, hydrate, run, repeat. Running long distances is one of the activities recommended for those who struggle with PTSD symptoms, as it prompts you to attune to your body, sensations, and needs. [85] The simplicity of energy management and focusing on moving forward one step at a time, mile after mile, makes everyday stressors seem so small in comparison. Around mile 20, I started feeling a lot of emotions. Some of the things we had been working on during EMDR that week came flooding back. I meditate and process issues while running, and the LSD removed some emotional barriers and heightened the emotions I was feeling.

For years now, I felt the innocent, naïve version of me that married at 18 was locked deep inside, crying and unable to be comforted. The younger me was still shocked and in disbelief about how everything turned out and how cruel the world could be. I kept thinking about that part of me. I thought a lot about the version of me that married at 18, believing everything would work out. Christians don't get divorced. Love and Jesus get you through. How could the person who swore to love and protect you become the monster that stalked your nightmares?

In EMDR that week, we had been working on this haunting memory I had about the time the kid's dad became explosively angry at our then 6-year-old daughter. When I intervened with his physical punishment, he lashed out at all of us, breaking and throwing things at me, raging in anger and out of control. I felt so ashamed to remember how, after he stormed off, I got mad at her, telling her she should know better than to make her dad angry. I then became upset at myself, knowing she was the child in this situation and it wasn't her fault.

Looking back, I felt so guilty for the times I got frustrated with her childish self for stomping all over the very obvious eggshells in our home. This memory is just one example of the cognitive dissonance that breaks the mind in an abusive relationship. While reprocessing, my therapist was trying to help me see the truth of my tenuous position in the family, doing the best I could to protect all of us. While running and thinking about how strongly I felt I couldn't save my baby girl, haunted by what we experienced, upset I couldn't protect us more, mad at myself we even ended up in that situation, I became overwhelmed and began crying on the trail. My stomach started cramping, and I felt very nauseous. The mind has heightened susceptibility to emotions when pushed past comfortable endurance, and the LSD opened me up even more.

A few miles later, I came to an aid station where my mom waited to run with me. I must have looked green because the aid volunteers took one look at me and began throwing water and ginger my way. We set off again together, and her company for the rest of the race lifted my spirits. Around mile 27, I got uncomfortably hot. To this day, I'm not sure if it was an unseasonably warm winter day (we were running in full sun at this point) or if I was experiencing flushing from extra serotonin. We stopped at every creek crossing to cool off; at one point, my mom was even sitting in the snowmelt stream. *(If she was hot, too, it couldn't have been the LSD. Right?)* We finished the race together. I had made a little more progress with processing my past but decided to run without LSD during future events.

By far, the most healing experiences have been with just Les and me, talking all night and sometimes all the next day about anything and everything. One night, we decided to try 400 mcg. I wanted to see if the higher dose would be similar to mushrooms in helping my mind piece together some profound life questions and healing wounded areas. As the LSD peaked, I had a feeling of crawling out of my body as my nerves came alive. I asked myself why I sought these experiences and had some nausea. My mind struggled to talk to Les and stay connected, wanting to drift off somewhere deep inside. At the same time, my thoughts were connecting faster than I could process, drawing conclusions and rushing on to the next topic before I could fully integrate my thoughts or even share them with Les. I tried to hold on to the revelations that meant the most to me.

We discussed Christianity, faith, and love. As we talked, I asked myself if I could fulfill the requirements of Christianity, the law, and the prophets with love. I comprehended I could. The greatest command is to love God and love others. I asked myself if I could do that and realized from deep within that I could. I felt a massive sense of relief. Les said something I will never forget, "Jesus came offering radical love and acceptance, and all He asked in return was for us to love in return. Love God and love others." My soul responded with a profound yes, finally something I *could* do! A standard I could live up to!

As we have explored my faith in EMDR, I realized I have always felt I can't measure up. This feeling is so overwhelming I walked away from Christianity altogether. The bar was always higher, no matter what I did. We attended church events almost every day, I read my Bible and prayed daily, I volunteered countless hours at the church, we went door to door to tell others about Jesus, we fasted and prayed for days, and I still felt I wasn't good enough. Church leaders told us to strive harder, do more, and be better Christians.

At the same time, I was drowning in acute feelings of inadequacy and imperfection. I was depressed and hated myself. I left an abusive marriage, and after I remarried another Christian, I was told I committed adultery. No matter what I did, I always failed as a Christian. I was raised with a very conditional version of Jesus' love. God loves me if I did everything I was supposed to as a Christian. If I didn't, then even though He loves me, He will send me to Hell. The people I went to church with radically loved and accepted everyone unless the person walked away from the church, and then we were treated like we didn't exist, or worse, were a bad influence and should be cut off. I'm Type A and a perfectionist. I tried harder and harder until I gave up under the weight of my failings.

As we discussed Hell and the wrath of God, it hit me that if I believe in all of the terror and anger of God to such an unimaginable extent, then all of the good parts of God, like grace, mercy, forgiveness, and love, are also indescribably huge. In my heart, I realized I could cast myself on the beautiful parts of God. If we can't fathom how horrible Hell is, then we also can't fathom how deep and genuine God loves and forgives us. When my mind turned to terror, I reminded myself of the unending mercy and kindness of God.

For the first time, my soul felt like it could rest. Inside, there was always this little kid cowering and praying for forgiveness, terrified beyond description of being thrown into Hell, but also not able to live the life of rules. Now, I keep coming back to love. The answer to everything was love. I held on to the imagery that God created and loved jellyfish, and they just float through the ocean, chillin'. The jellyfish just be. And God loves them and calls them beautiful. My soul can rest and be.

We compared religions of the world. What if Christianity isn't true? What if some other belief is true? After all, I am gambling my very soul on these beliefs. I kept coming back to love. If I could love God and love others, I would fulfill the basic tenets of most belief systems. I looked at this concept from every angle. Was there a downside to striving to live a life of love? I couldn't find a downside. However, I did feel the need for balance because, as someone who survived domestic violence, sometimes love says no. I asked myself repeatedly if I could live a life of love, and would this be the life I wanted to live? The resounding answer was yes.

We talked about generational trauma. Somehow, I could look at every person who ever hurt me and see factors leading to their hurtful actions. I could follow it back generation after generation, seeing the woundedness and pain spilling from generation to generation. I saw my first husband and the pain and brokenness he caused the kids and me. As I looked further, I could see how he had been hurt and broken as a child, and then before him, I saw those who harmed and broke his parents. In many ways, I saw that he never stood a chance either.

In turn, I thought about those I hurt. I felt so guilty, circling over and over to the things I could have done better. How did my actions impact others? My kids? My mind followed ripples, thinking back to hurt, causing more widespread societal hurt. And then we comprehended that, in the end, it didn't matter; everyone was hurt, and most were broken. Each generation causes hurt and passes on pain to the next generation. At some point, someone has to say no more. We can use our hurt as an excuse to cause more hurt or say it stops with us. We can shield the next generation, feeling the pain but not passing on that pain. All I can do about the past is forgive myself and try to improve daily. I was struck by how important it is for me to set a different example for my kids. We can't change the world, but we can improve our little part. And maybe love will be contagious, spreading from one tiny group to another.

I forgave. I could see ripples of pain experienced by myself and others. I recognize all of us are hurt to some extent, and being hurt doesn't justify hurting others. Still, it helped me empathize with difficult people, and I chose to forgive all over again. I refused to carry the weight of bitterness or unforgiveness forward in my life.

The weight of turning 40 soon struck me. I saw all the years behind me, decades of hurt and pain, years I never wanted to live again. I saw my life with Les spreading before me, and for once, the time seemed short. I had never felt so wholly accepted and loved by another human being. The importance of thoughtfully moving forward and wisely choosing how I want to spend the remaining time impacted me.

I realized I had been waiting for someone older, wiser, to fix the wrong things in life, to make sense of the insensible. I saw the family secrets loved ones didn't discuss from generation to generation. I observed people living lives they didn't want to live, resulting in feelings of bitterness and regret. I struggled with the societal pressure that we should stay in certain situations and marriages, hating life and wishing it was different but hoping our sacrifice would please God and eternity would be happy instead. I made up my mind to live differently.

Previous generations have made their choices; for the sake of my mental health and my kids, I have to do it differently. I'm not perfect, but I can be honest. I can be transparent in not knowing what to do, in my mistakes, and in trying to grow and change. I don't have it all figured out, but I can offer a place of healing and acceptance for all of us to learn together. I discerned the individuals in our family and friend groups who were struggling, hurting, and down, and felt an overwhelming urge to try to reach out, connect, and help. We both felt a strong desire to help others find healing and peace.

Along with all the seriousness, we became a younger, sillier version of ourselves. We listened to music for hours, singing, dancing *(be glad you weren't there!)*, and talking. We realized that even our 5-year-old selves loved each other. We remembered memories we hadn't thought about in years. Finding someone to be silly and laugh with was so freeing—a fun sleepover with a super sexy bestie. As Anne Shulgin perfectly described it, "Children live in the world we visit with psychedelics."[66]

Our everyday lives are grave, with a lot of leadership responsibilities. We are parents, friends, and co-workers with people who depend on us daily. Life is a lot of pressure. LSD allowed us the freedom to return to a lighter version of ourselves. I carried this lightened version of life back into everyday life. Things often aren't as serious as we take them.

Thoughts from EMDR: September 2023

Being a GOOD mom is different than being a PERFECT mom.

Thoughts from EMDR: October 2023

There were so many holes in the walls and doors. Why was I always the one fixing those? Why was I the one who was embarrassed? The holes I couldn't patch had pretty pictures over them.

The past seems like another life now. Some days, it's hard to believe it all happened. Some days, I want to hug the younger me. I am so grateful for my life now; it is worth anything I have lost or paid to live in love and peace.

Dosage and Effects

Due to the wide range of doses and effects of LSD, the onset, peak, and duration of LSD listed is regarding a 100 to 200 microgram dose. As doses increase, you may experience longer durations of effects.

Onset: 1 to 2 hours

Peak: 2 to 4 hours

Duration: 6 to 12 hours

Low Dose/Microdose (25 to 75 mcg):

LSD is perceptible down to about 25 micrograms, where the effects are very mild. The effects are mild but noticeable in the 50 to 75 micrograms dose range. After our initial experimentation, we have been primarily taking 100 micrograms or more of LSD due to that being our threshold for the effects we most enjoy.

Mood Effects: Slightly enhanced mood and sensory perception are possible. Mild emotional intensification, potentially leading to either euphoria or increased anxiety.

Visual/Sensory Effects: You might experience slight visual alterations, such as brighter colors and enhanced patterns. Any visual effects are very light, if perceptible at all.

Touch Effects: Feeling more connected to one's own body or surroundings is possible. Touch sensations increase.

Physical Effects: Expect minor increases in heart rate and blood pressure. One may experience mild dizziness or nausea.

Moderate Low Dose (75 to 150 Micrograms):

75 to 150 micrograms is a great dose to enhance an experience. It is also the range where you can interact with normies without them suspecting too much.

Mood Effects: You may experience an uplifted, even joyful mood at this dose range. While not as common as in the higher doses, you may ponder deep thoughts and reflect on life.

Visual/Sensory Effects: You might experience subtle visual hallucinations, including geometric patterns and objects that may "breathe." We want to emphasize that these effects are pretty mild and are not intrusive or interfering with activities.

Touch Effects: You may feel that touch is slightly enhanced and that when things or people touch you, your skin is usually more sensitive, in a good way.

Physical Effects: You will start to feel an energy boost and have energy for conversations, movement, and sensual activities. Remember your duration of effect because that is how long you will be awake. Taking LSD at 11:00 p.m. will result in an all-night trip. Expect to be hot and cold as your body will be hard-pressed to keep your temperature regular. You may alternately sweat or shiver, regardless of the outside temperature. And, speaking of outside temperature, be careful if you are doing anything strenuous because you may overheat and become dehydrated. Regular activity should be acceptable if you are hydrated, but running or hiking a gnarly trail could overheat you.

Moderate-High Dose (150 to 250 Micrograms):

200 micrograms can be great for socializing, attending concerts, or spending time out in nature. If desired, this dose allows you to feel some effects while participating in everyday activities. Peak at these doses can be intrusive, so pick an inconspicuous time to try it out for the first time.

Mood Effects: Your emotions will be more pronounced, with exaggerated feelings. Watch for your set and setting because if you feel unsafe or anxious, these emotions will also increase. As the doses increase, you will think more about life and more profound existential ponderings.

Visual/Sensory Effects: Depending on your sensitivity, you may experience visual hallucinations, with patterns, colors, fractals, and "breathing" objects possible. Marked alterations in the perception of time are a fun feature as well. You might find that it feels like no time has passed, but several hours have flown by. Taste and smell can be enhanced profoundly, with food, candles, and even hand soap freshly impacting your senses.

Touch Effects: Touch and feel will be much more sensitive. Your skin can become very sensitive. Sexual activities, depending on the couple, can be enhanced greatly.

Physical Effects: You will experience a substantial body high that might include fine tremors (like when you drink too much coffee), jaw clenching, nausea, vertigo, temperature deregulation, or sweating.

High Dose (250 to 350 Micrograms):

This is the highest dose range we recommend for individuals or couples who still want to be able to talk and interact. If you or your partner are very sensitive to psychedelics, this dose might be too high if you are trying to avoid traveling inside yourself. Starting at these doses, you may be thinking about things differently. Everything you do may result in it feeling novel and new. You might make new connections about things in your life or even discover novel solutions to your problems.

Mood Effects: Depending on your set and setting, emotional experiences may be overwhelming and profound, ranging from euphoria to fear. You may resolve some spiritual or emotional issues due to your thoughts and conversation.

Visual/Sensory Effects: Again, depending on your sensitivity to visuals with psychedelics, you may experience intensely vivid and encompassing visual hallucinations. We don't have profound visuals at this dose, but we have sensitive friends who have. This dose may not allow much socialization for the sensitive and acts as more of an internal journey. We highly recommend music because your favorite songs will sound much better. Even music you aren't into will sound incredible as if it was composed for listening on LSD. Your taste and smell are enhanced, and while this can go both ways, we find that foods generally taste delicious.

Touch Effects: As your other senses are overwhelmed, touch is enhanced but will not be the focus. Your other senses are dialed up to 11, and the touch senses won't keep up. After the peak, when you are on the comedown, you may still have a lot of that MDMA-like skin sensitivity. That is a great time to connect with your partner.

Physical Effects: One can expect an increase in heart rate, blood pressure, and temperature deregulation at this dose. You run a higher risk of unpleasant physical symptoms, including severe nausea, internal restlessness, tremors, shaking, and jaw clenching. Some people don't like the body high at these doses, but if you can endure those symptoms, the experiences overall can be awe-inspiring.

Very High Dose (400 Micrograms+):

Mood Effects: Expect extremely intense emotional states, which can be euphoric and distressing. This dose has a high potential for profound and overwhelming existential experiences.

Visual/Sensory Effects: Anticipate incredibly immersive and often intense visual experiences with the potential for losing the sense of self and surroundings.

Touch Effects: These doses lead to an utterly altered sense of touch and even a feeling of dissolving or becoming one with the environment.

Physical Effects: Dramatic physical responses are normal, including very high heart rate, blood pressure, and a risk of overheating. There is a heightened risk of severe physical discomfort and disorientation.

Health, Safety, and Addiction

LSD is considered relatively safe due to one's inability to die as a result of an overdose and its low toxicity to the body. Even in a psychological context, LSD seems to have a high level of safety despite the propaganda to the contrary.

The LD50 of LSD in humans is not known, as there are no known deaths by overdose. In mice, the LD50 is 16.5mg/Kg, 16,500 mcg of acid. [7] One incident involved eight individuals who mistakenly snorted powdered LSD, mistaking it for cocaine, and were hospitalized. The amount of LSD in their blood, when sampled, was 1000-7000 micrograms per 100 mL of blood. For reference, the human body has 4500-5500 mL of blood, meaning they consumed a *lot* of LSD.

The effects of LSD during pregnancy are not fully understood, but several studies have shown that there are no negative effects during pregnancy. That said, LSD has not been thoroughly studied, and its use during pregnancy is not something we can endorse in any way.

People commonly reference anecdotes of psychosis and suicidality. Still, in the over 10,000 participants in LSD studies, the rates of these types of complications are the same as the adverse effects associated with psychotherapy. [10] LSD is not recommended for individuals with psychotic disorders, though little research on this exists as well.

In our combined 20-year history of working in substance abuse and mental health, we have never seen anyone in treatment for an LSD addiction. Interestingly, it is also quite rare to find LSD on a patient's list of "other drugs" they have a history of using regularly. LSD, like all psychedelics used frequently, results in a tolerance that severely limits any effects of subsequent doses. We have tried using LSD 2 nights in a row, and the second night's dose was nearly imperceptible. So, don't be too concerned about addiction, but like anything, addictive behavior can form around anything.

Medication/Drug Interactions:

We recommend you discuss any psychedelic use while on prescription medications with your physician or pharmacist.

Cannabis- As with all psychedelics, cannabis has a strong and unpredictable synergy with psychedelics. As a force multiplier, remember that not only will the "positive" effects of the psychedelic be heightened. If combined, use much smaller doses of both substances and go slow.

Lithium- As a common psychiatric medication, Lithium has been reported to increase the risk of seizures and psychosis. Combining Lithium with any psychedelic is **strongly discouraged**!

Amphetamines/Cocaine- All psychedelics become dangerous when mixed with amphetamines and cocaine. These are addictive and can cause Serotonin Syndrome, a life-threatening condition.

Antidepressants (SSRIs)- SSRIs (e.g., Celexa, Prozac, Lexapro, Paxil) are suspected to increase the risk for Serotonin Syndrome, a potentially life-threatening condition. Still, research shows that SSRIs are low risk for this complication. Of note, a study of Serotonin Syndrome cases associated with MDMA found that all 20 cases were the result of mixing MDMA with amphetamines, cocaine, or opioids. [42] Last, there is frequent anecdotal reporting of antidepressants decreasing the felt effects of MDMA.

Tramadol- A prescription pain medication, it is known that Tramadol reduces the seizure threshold when combined with serotonergic drugs (e.g., all psychedelics) and also increases the risk for Serotonin Syndrome. [40]

Les's Story

Ahhh, LSD, how I love thee. LSD has many faces, including the intellectual, philosopher, musician, dancer, comedian, child, and so much more. I have found a lot of clarity after discussing spirituality, life, and everything with Byrd and our close friends. Acid allows the mind to bend and flex in ways that weren't possible before, making intuitive jumps to solve the conundrums of my heart and mind.

At higher doses (300-400mcg), I have found that LSD allows me to access memories lost to me for many years. Remembering events from when I was 2 or 3 is hilarious to share, but they are also like reuniting parts of myself. They have helped me understand myself and accept those parts I didn't understand well. Here is one memory that is a favorite of mine and our whole family:

I don't know my exact age, but it was while living in Phoenix, Arizona, before moving to Saudi Arabia. That would make me 2 or 3 at the time. My mom, always seeking some new social hobby, decided that her son was cute enough to be in pageants. So, Les joined the baby/toddler beauty pageant circuit for a time. I'm sure you have seen the Dance Mom shows and the intensity of these mothers, but my mother was not. My mom had a carefree attitude that wasn't pressuring or overbearing. If she had, this whole endeavor would have failed before it started.

I was adorable, precocious, sassy, and could connect instantly with adults, especially women. My mom would do my hair, dress me in adorable "little man's" clothing, and send me on stage without any talents or plans. I was a natural, blowing kisses to the judges, making eye contact, smiling, and being well-spoken *(for a three-year-old)*. Needless to say, I did very well on the Central Phoenix beauty pageant circuit. My closet contained the ribbons, awards, and trophies of my time as "Pageant Les." *(Until one day as an awkward 12-year-old when those had to go!)* One of those trophies was 3 or 4 feet tall, representing the triumphant end to my short career.

I was one of the only boys entering into these pageants. *(I wish I could ask my dad how he felt about this)*. Most girls had intense moms trying to cajole their toddlers into doing whatever dance or talent routine they had been drilling into them. You can probably imagine their anger at losing to a cute, tan-skinned, green-eyed little boy with no talents. I remember walking through a parking lot after winning a show, feeling the glares and anger of these "dance moms." I loved it. To this day, there is a bit of attitude, flare, and sass in my personality.

After LSD dredged up this memory, I shared it with my daughters. For my oldest, it has become her favorite "dad story." My girls are quick-witted and sassy, able to hold their own against adults. People wrongly assume they got this sass from their mother. Nope, they get their flare for the dramatic and quick wit from their dad, Pageant Les.

While the "Pageant Les" story is a favorite of my girls, Byrd included, it connected me to a part of myself that I never really understood. That memory helped me to understand who I have always been, even as a toddler.

Another fascinating benefit of LSD has been the ability to organize and understand my spirituality while being the vigorous Christian apologist Byrd needs. Byrd's story about her struggles with finding her true faith, despite the twisted tenets of a fundamentalist church built into her since birth, pushed me to organize my thoughts on faith and Christianity despite not being a Christian myself.

When Byrd and I met, I was reluctant to accept Christianity in any way. My messed-up childhood had a religious undertone that, once I left the church, left a bad taste in my mouth. As a longtime friend of Byrd's, I understood how her faith was the one shelter from the storm available to her, and at the same time, the twisted teachings of that faith were some of the strongest elements of that storm.

Through our many discussions on LSD, psilocybin, and MDMA/MDA, we have both found a sense of peace in our spirituality. I often tease Byrd that it's hilarious that her only non-Christian partner, me, is the strongest and most balanced supporter of her Christian faith. My experience with shrooms changed forever how I look at religion and spirituality. We all seek the same God but through the many faces of God. For me, it is the Earth Mother, likely a remnant of my pagan Irish roots. For Byrd, it is Christ. God always asks us to love people, love God, and love ourselves. If you live by those tenets, I believe you fulfill God's purpose for us.

LSD is deep and shallow, making it fun and insightful. I have had some of the most significant mental breakthroughs on LSD while also having some of the funniest nights of my life on that same substance. It mixes amazingly with MDMA/MDA, extending trips that would typically only span 6 to 10 hours for 18 to 24 hours. An 18-hour trip has a way of stripping away everything and leaving you in a beautiful, childlike state. After discovering this childlike state one night, Byrd and I concluded that five-year-old Byrd also loves 5-year-old Les.

Home Rolling

Using LSD at home is a real treat. We have thoroughly enjoyed taking 100 to 400 micrograms at home, just the two of us, or with friends. With the length of the high associated with LSD, it is essential to be mindful of the time since you will be awake for 12 hours and acutely high for 6 to 8 hours. At the lower doses, your mindset is not as critical, but be aware that if you have a lot on your mind or heart, you might be processing this at some point with your partner or friends.

As far as the setting is concerned, make yourself a comfortable little nest with beverages, snacks, and music. Another great addition to your setting, if a TV or projector is available, is to search YouTube for psychedelic videos. With the advancement of AI art, the psychedelic video space has boomed with amazing videos for your tripping pleasure. See some of our recommended trip videos at the end of this book.

Use in Therapy

LSD does not have widespread use in therapy found in some other classic psychedelics, but that is not a reflection of its usefulness in the therapy space. A recent study of individuals with and without life-threatening illnesses found that there was a significant reduction in anxiety and depression following treatment with 200 micrograms of LSD. [11] The participants had continued reduction of anxiety and depression immediately following the first treatment and at 16 weeks after treatment. These results were nearly identical to those in psilocybin research focusing on the same population. While research is slowly coming forward, it appears that LSD is as valuable as other psychedelics in the treatment of mental health disorders. Time will tell if LSD is better or different than other classic psychedelics like psilocybin.

Takeaways

If your stomach is sensitive, take an over-the-counter medication before LSD. The body-high sensations usually only last 30 minutes or so, and afterward, it's all worth it.

Lower doses of LSD are sociable; higher doses become more introspective.

Lower doses allow you to walk around, higher doses affect equilibrium, and you will want to sit or lie down.

Processing is best done with someone else *(but not during a party!)*.

LSD is hands down the best substance for listening to music and is recommended for concerts any day. *(It also makes lights look fantastic!)*

LSD brings out your inner child. *(Our friends have reported this, too.)*

After the peak, LSD makes food taste *so good*! That neuroplasticity works on food, too, and your brain exclaims in delight that whatever you're eating has never tasted so good, seriously, ever! *(Best McDonald's of my life... just saying!)*

Support the right to consciousness!

KETAMINE: A LEGAL PSYCHEDELIC

Introduction

Discussing ketamine as a psychedelic is somewhat controversial; however, the research into ketamine with depression treatment demonstrates unmistakable psychedelic behaviors at specific doses. Before we start, ketamine is not a "couples' drug" in the sense we have discussed MDMA and LSD, but ketamine is a medicine we have used together on our journey of healing.

Our focus in this chapter will be solely on the therapeutic use of ketamine for the treatment of depression and anxiety due to the risks associated with regular and long-term use. Ketamine is highly effective in the treatment of depression and suicidality and should be used for those purposes, even at home.

We DO NOT support the use of ketamine as a recreational drug; it is medicine. Ketamine used inappropriately can lead to death. We chose to include this substance in our book because of its incredible ability to treat depression and suicidality. That said, if you choose to use ketamine, proceed with caution. Ketamine is legally used to treat depression, and there are clinics available in many locations for this purpose. Ketamine is highly unique because this medicine can be obtained legally as a treatment for mood, depression, pain, addiction, PTSD, and suicidal thoughts. There are now many clinics in the U.S. open and available for treatment if you are struggling in these areas. We HIGHLY recommend finding a clinic that combines ketamine with integration, coaching or therapy for the best results.

History

Ketamine was first synthesized in 1962 as a derivative of another pain medication in the hopes of creating a medication with a shorter action. Still, they were surprised by the results of the new substance as it caused a unique mental state while also having profound pain relieving and sedative effects. The first patients to experience the "K-hole," or dissociative effects, reported feeling they were in outer space or that they had no arms and legs. [12]

Psychiatry found ketamine in the 1970s, with research published on its use in the treatment of various mental maladies. During these early years, no definitive works were published, and ketamine remained a fringe drug in psychiatry. In the 1980s and 1990s, Dr. Krupitsky conducted groundbreaking research on the use of ketamine, in conjunction with therapy, to treat addiction. His research on heroin addiction highlights the benefits of ketamine in the addiction and recovery space. Among heroine-addicted participants who underwent three ketamine treatments with therapy, 50% were sober at one-year post-treatment. [14] Compare Krupitsky's results to the standard results found in traditional drug rehab programs (even the ones for the rich), where 5 to 8% sobriety at one year is expected.

In the new millennium, the first randomized-controlled studies showing ketamine's apparent effects in the treatment of depression were published. [13] These works formed the basis for the recent FDA approval of Spravato (esketamine) and the use of ketamine in clinics across the country treating depression.

Of particular interest to us, ketamine treats people who are actively suicidal. A single dose of ketamine reduces depression in suicidal individuals enough that they can be discharged home instead of being admitted to a psychiatric hospital. *(How flipping cool is that?)* Byrd remembers times when she was afraid to seek help because she didn't want to be involuntarily committed and didn't want untrue accusations of being an unfit parent compounding her already complex parenting situation. Imagine if people could ask for help without fear of being stigmatized or sent inpatient against their will.

Legal Status

Ketamine is not a Schedule I substance. *(For once, I get to say this!)* Ketamine is a Schedule III drug. So, it is still controlled and illegal to abuse, but it is in the same category as Testosterone and Tylenol with Codeine. Be careful still, as it is not legal to possess ketamine without a prescription.

Byrd's Story

My depression had improved a lot, and I went weeks without thinking about killing myself. I sometimes started rating my depression as 0 when I went into EMDR therapy. However, there were still days I struggled or lost myself and sat there staring into space, trying to keep myself above the emotional waves. I apologized for my lack of energy and wanting to lie down, watch a movie, and forget the world. Les kept me grounded. He is my home. Every time I left, I counted the moments until we were back together. How could the world feel so much less overwhelming and downright doable when he held me?

EMDR was hard work. Some days, I had to force myself to go. I knew I would feel much worse after every session. My emotional walls are so high I don't feel sad about anything that has happened when I'm going about my typical day. EMDR inevitably takes me behind the walls built around my emotions, leaving me feeling more down than when I arrived. That said, little by little, I could see progress. At my darkest times, my mind would fixate on thoughts like "I'm a bad mom. I'm a bad Christian. I'm a bad wife. I should have done this or that differently. How did I end up here? How could I let all of this happen?" From there, my thoughts deteriorated until I felt only despair and hopelessness and concluded I should die. EMDR silenced the mental loops I would get stuck in one by one. We tackled everything from my panicked reactions about weight and negative body image to specific moments of trauma and the negative beliefs associated with each memory.

I wanted to get off depression medication. I hate feeling like I have to take something and that something is wrong with me. Side effects like getting a headache when I forget to take a dose are annoying. I had heard and read about ketamine and decided if my depression worsened, I would pay the money for a full six sessions of IV infusions. Even a single down day caused me to feel panicked inside. What if the depression was coming back? What if I couldn't stop it? I didn't want to be a burden to anyone, and I didn't want to live with the overwhelming emotional pain.

My psychiatric NP agreed to prescribe intranasal ketamine for depression. My insurance would cover the intranasal (esketamine), but IV ketamine would be out of pocket and likely cost thousands of dollars. My NP related some patients were able to stop depression medication after receiving ketamine, others were able to decrease, and others were still on medication but experienced better relief from symptoms of depression. Each appointment would require someone else to drive me home. While considering the options, Les was able to locate ketamine we could take at home. I had read so much about the benefits of ketamine I was hopeful this would significantly improve my depression, maybe permanently.

Ketamine can be self-administered in many ways, including intranasal, oral, IV, IM, as an enema, and subcutaneously. The first time we took ketamine, we self-administered 75 mg intranasally. It was a subtherapeutic dose, but I wanted to work my way up slowly. I felt a little dizzy but didn't notice any other effects. We self-administered 100 mg the next time, which I felt a little more, but not much. The next dose was 150 mg, and eventually 200 mg. I don't love its taste or feeling in my nose or the back of my throat. At the higher doses, the medication kicked in within 10 minutes, and I felt dizzy with light sensitivity, making me want to close my eyes. Each time we lay down together, so no matter how I felt during the experience, I could feel Les close to me.

Ketamine overwhelms the mind, making thoughts sifting sand, freely flowing through your mind. On the days when I felt depressed and took ketamine, I was unable to hold on tightly to the thoughts making me sad. The thoughts would flow away, leading to other thoughts and then another, too many to hold on to by the end of the experience. Ketamine has an overall happy and uplifting feeling. Even if I delved into issues that brought me to tears, overall, my mood improved.

One of the first things I felt as ketamine kicked in was my lips would become numb; from there, other parts of my body would start to feel distant from myself, like when a limb fell asleep from sitting in one position too long. Ketamine powerfully distorts the sense of reality, but at the same time, I could always open my eyes and reorient myself to where I was or touch Les and know he was there. When my eyes are closed, I can faintly see shapes moving behind my eyelids, but closing my eyes tighter or wearing an eye mask doesn't bring the shapes into greater focus or brighten the colors. It's always a faint movie playing behind my eyes.

The shapes behind my eyelids move and change to the music. We have always heard music is essential as ketamine distorts time, and silence can be highly disorienting while on ketamine. Once, a loud motorcycle went by outside, and the exhaust sound seemed to come in waves and last forever. Sometimes, my thoughts are moving so fast that I have entire thought streams between two beats of the music. I learned that music selection is crucial. Once the ketamine kicks in fully, I can't focus my eyes enough to change my phone or switch songs. A couple of times, the music that came on was too slow or had a sad mood or connotation, and I struggled to maintain positive emotions.

Eventually, we transitioned to listening to soundtracks created for ketamine without words. While I was skeptical at first, after trying music without lyrics and then switching back to my favorite popular songs, I appreciated that the music without words enhanced the experience by allowing my mind to go where it wanted to go instead of constantly being swept into and overwhelmed by the next track that played.

When ketamine begins to peak, the thoughts sweep along and away. I felt my mind pulled out of the sad loops, and I could not fixate on despair or hopeless thoughts. Later, I learned this was ketamine turning off my Default Mode Network. Knowing the problems that can arise from fighting a trip, I consciously instructed myself to let go and go with the flow. One of the first times, I had the overwhelming feeling my mind was taking me to Hell, similar to when I tried the heroic dose of mushrooms. Instead of feeling sheer terror this time, I felt three streams flowing in my inner core. One was still the sheer terror of Hell, one was my belief in Jesus, and the third was my belief in love, especially the unimaginable love of God. I felt these three things in equal parts at my center and chose to flow with my faith in Jesus and love. This trip happened about a year after the experience with the heroic dose of mushrooms, and I felt confirmation of how far I had come in the healing process.

Ketamine lends to a feeling of the mind dancing to music. The thoughts flow and move you down a river along with the medicine. As the medicine takes off, there's a sensation of going over a waterfall and being caught in the current. At times, it was like I was distinctly separate from my mind and could watch parts of my mind conversing with each other, debating issues back and forth. Other times, I could feel my mind making new connections; my neurons were growing and entwining in new ways. I had unusual thought connections, like seeing myself with my young daughter riding in my truck and then myself with my stepdaughter riding in Les's truck, and somehow, my mind was putting these memories together like one long stream.

I felt pulled out of myself several times, up and away from the Earth. I was looking back and realizing just how small everything and everyone was. Why was I stressing out about these little details that didn't matter? The circumstances that overwhelmed me suddenly felt put into perspective. Then, I felt overwhelmed by sheer fun and happiness; I saw myself dancing through life, sitting at a work meeting, and a dance party broke out. I decided life is way too severe and should involve more dancing. Why are we taking this so seriously when life can be fun and is terribly short?

I thought of some projects I was trying to manage at work. I felt overwhelmed by the tasks ahead of me, and in some ways, the significant changes seemed improbable. I felt so tired, and then a few moments later, I felt warm and sunny, thinking how outstanding the outcomes would be, and it made it worth it. I thought of some of the complex situations at work, and it all seemed minor and unimportant. All that mattered was helping others. I felt myself letting go of negative and painful emotions and instead focusing on what we could do to heal others. I felt love flowing out of me and into the world.

I struggled with how to protect myself and others who unkind people were hurting. My mind tried to balance the dissonance of loving and reaching out in kindness while also protecting myself and those who are vulnerable. I found myself willing to be kind and loving, strong, and able to say no and stand up for those who are downtrodden.

During this time, I visited my family out of state, celebrating my brother's retirement from the military. It was a very emotional time, filled with tentative reconnection, healing, and hope for better relationships. Les and I self-administered ketamine after we got back home. During the experience, my mind connected for the first time how I felt like I couldn't protect my younger brother from various difficult circumstances growing up and how this related to a similar feeling with my kids later in my life.

I felt the pull between being in the church and my brother leaving the church, and I recognized how the church contributed to the strain on our relationship going back a long time. My brother and I had a complicated relationship for a long time, and now I can more clearly see where each of us was coming from and empathize with him and what he experienced. I felt an overwhelming urge to reconnect with my brother. The following day, I texted him, acknowledging that I was deconstructing a lot right now and apologizing for my role in losing our relationship. I told him how much I loved him and was so proud of him and the man he had become. We exchanged texts of love and reconciliation for the first time in years.

A psychologist told me it was helpful to set an intention before each ketamine experience. I began asking my mind what I needed to heal each time I took ketamine. During one experience, after I started setting intentions, I re-engaged some questions about my faith. My mind was contemplating different aspects of the Bible and God. I remembered an experience in middle school that I look back on with great embarrassment. Our history teacher asked us to invent a tribe and write about the people, the laws, and their society.

I based my tribe on Old Testament Israel. I distinctly remember writing about how if a woman divorced her husband, she should be stoned. *(The kind where they throw rocks at you until you die, not the kind that involves a lot of marijuana!)* I remember one of my friends from church telling me how she wrote about her tribe wearing cool armbands. Even then, I remember feeling embarrassed that something was off. Why was I writing about divorcees being stoned in 7th grade? I felt ashamed.

Then, in my mind, I became the woman who was divorced, and I was being stoned. I kept thinking that would be me now, twice divorced. I felt the rocks falling on me. Then I was pulled back, and now I was God watching this scene, and these were my people, and my heart broke. Why were my people hurting each other? For any reason? Why??? I didn't want that, and I didn't want my people hurting each other. I also felt great empathy, forgiveness, and mercy for my young self, all the way back in 7th grade, parroting what I was taught. Black and white was all I knew back then. Having lived a broken life, I now see only shades of gray in every person and situation. I am learning to extend forgiveness to myself along with others.

We experimented with IM ketamine instead of intranasal and once tried a ketamine enema. The enema gave me terrible lower intestinal cramps, but otherwise, it didn't make the experience any different. The IM ketamine hits the same every time. Intranasal ketamine sometimes doesn't fully take effect, and there have been times I have read or watched a movie the entire experience. Incidentally, one of these times, I was feeling highly stressed and later wondered if my body reacting to stress was preventing the full effect of the ketamine.

Compared with intranasal, IM ketamine takes effect with a much quicker rise to the peak and drop at the end. The results between the IM and intranasal were broadly similar, aside from how fast the peak rose at the beginning and tapered at the end. Ketamine is a medication that takes you deep internally. During the experience, we didn't talk; sometimes, we couldn't talk even if we wanted to.

Ketamine is personalized and unique to each person and does not generate a connective bonding experience between us. That said, there have been times when a ketamine experience lowered our emotional defenses, and afterward, we freely discussed issues we needed to talk about. When Les has self-administered ketamine without me, we will talk about his experience after and any insights he has gained. However, it does not lend to a feeling of enhanced connection.

Sometimes, I feel so emotionally exhausted after ketamine that I struggle to find words to talk about the experience for a bit. When both of us are taking ketamine, we are immersed in our own experiences, and it can be a struggle to try and integrate while also being present for the other person. Suppose one person self-administers ketamine, and the other is present for support and an integrative discussion afterward. This approach will allow the partners to experience and support each other along their healing journey.

Of course, we tried having sex on ketamine, not frequently but once or twice. Once, we had become disconnected and disagreed about some minor issues. As soon as the ketamine started peaking, the medicine removed everything holding us apart. We started holding each other, remembering how little the minor annoyances compared with the importance of just being together, and one thing led to another. It was a unique sexual experience, unlike any other substance. My body felt numb in parts, while other parts registered enhanced touch and contact. My brain encountered sex like it was a whole new experience. I wanted to be as close as possible to Les. Overall, the experience was short and fun. However, we prefer MDMA when it comes to enhancing physical touch.

After stabilizing on thyroid medication, I started semaglutide for weight loss. Unfortunately, I became very sick the first time I used ketamine after starting the semaglutide. I threw up several times, felt a burning sensation in my head, and struggled with distorted reality while also feeling desperately ill. The whole time, my mind was screaming ketamine was a terrible decision and I was going to die. The time distortion made me feel like I was sick for hours when, in actuality, it was about an hour. I decided to wait on any further doses of ketamine until finishing the course of semaglutide.

I continued the semaglutide until I regained my pre-Hashimoto body weight and then stopped. I was able to decrease my antidepressant dose by 50% but was unable to stop the medication entirely at that time.

Ketamine is medicine. This drug is not for fun, and I can't understand how people use this substance when partying because the side effects make me feel dizzy, and I have to close my eyes. I really cannot understand how people use ketamine often and in significant enough amounts to develop an addiction. That said, I know experiences with substances in party settings are very different from home rolling, and while rare, there are cases of people addicted to ketamine after taking this medication frequently and in high doses.

Ketamine is powerful and effective in treating symptoms of acute and chronic depression. In my darkest times, ketamine could break the sad thought loops right away. Ketamine also boosted my mood from a few days to weeks after each administration.

While my life stressors remained high, ketamine gave me the ability to manage all the stress instead of feeling a need to escape.

Thoughts from EMDR: October 2023

You told me I couldn't possibly earn my way to heaven.

And then you handed me a list of actions that would get me thrown into Hell.

Cognitive dissonance.

I can never do enough to be in heaven, but there are any number of things I can do and find myself in Hell.

And so I gave up. I know me, and I know I can never be good enough. I can never do all the things you say I have to do.

So is it grace, or is it our work after all? How big is God's grace? How big is the love of God that I can lose it so easily? Why is it so hard to win?

I believe we haven't even begun to imagine the love, grace, kindness, and understanding of a God who would send His Son to die for us.

Dosage and Effects

As this is a home guide for couples, the dosages for ketamine will be for crystallized or powdered ketamine taken intranasally. Why intranasal administration? Oral ketamine requires much higher doses and has a much longer time-to-peak and duration, which are not desirable features for ketamine. Also, the ketamine available on the Dark Web or through street pharmacists is mostly in powder form, and we don't recommend using it to mix up a solution for injection for many reasons.

Ketamine is classified as a dissociative, meaning it can result in a disconnect between you and your body. Also, ketamine distorts hearing, sight, and time. As an anesthetic, you might notice that any pain you had going into the trip is decreased or gone altogether. The ultimate dissociative effect is commonly called the "K-hole," where you enter a complete state of dissociation that severely impairs your body's ability to move. The K-hole can be quite psychedelic, and one can find many insights in this state.

Dosing of ketamine can be split into two categories: psycholytic (no K-hole) and psychedelic (K-hole). Depending on your size and sensitivity, dosing between the two states of ketamine can vary. Our doses are similar to obtain the same effects, and our body weights have a 50-pound difference. We recommend starting low and moving up.

Onset: 5 to 10 minutes

Peak: 15 to 30 minutes

Duration: 45 to 55 minutes

Psycholytic Dosing (50 to 125 mg):

You should remain out of the K-hole in this dose range. Also, if the psychedelic dosing is too dramatic, some antidepressant effects can still be found in the sub-psychedelic dosing.

Mood Effects: You might feel a boost to your mood while feeling very chill and relaxed. As you near the K-Hole, you may have some feelings of anxiety or paranoia.

Visual and Sensory Effects: In the psycholytic dose range, you will likely not have any visual or other sensory disturbances.

Physical Body Effects: You might experience increased numbness and nausea as the dose increases. Use caution, as your ability to feel pain is significantly reduced.

Physical Activity: With the numbness and feeling of detachment from your body comes a potential challenge to moving about. Don't plan any acrobatics while using ketamine at these doses.

Psychedelic Dosing (125-250 mg):

Here, we enter the K-hole, and the "coupleness" of ketamine essentially ends, and your journey within begins. Remember, surrender to the experience. Ketamine at this dose is safe and will not kill you.

Like any highly psychedelic experience, the medicine sends you on a journey, and your job is to go along without fighting too hard.

Mood Effects: Ketamine has a very happy and overall positive vibe. You may feel anxiety if the visuals move too fast or get weird, but you won't get a sense of terror from the trip unless you fight it.

Visual and Sensory Effects: The visuals can be vivid, varied, and wild. We haven't experienced "bad" visuals on our trips, but they can get weird. For example, Les frequently has visuals where he dives into objects/scenery and travels into their atomic matter before changing into something else altogether.

One bizarre effect of dissociation is its impact on the perception of time. Music, which is a must for psychedelic ketamine trips, can stretch endlessly. Pauses between songs extend for minutes, and even the space between musical notes can be perceived.

Physical Body Effects: Expect to be fully numb and still in the K-hole. We find ourselves needing to get settled real quick after ingesting ketamine because we won't move for another 45 minutes. Your breathing will slow, but ketamine at these moderate doses will not cause respiratory complications. Also, while you may feel like you are in a coma-like state, you will have complete control over bodily functions.

Physical Activity: Nope. Get comfy; you aren't moving for 45 to 60 minutes.

Health Risk, Safety, and Addiction

Ketamine requires more caution than other medicines covered in this book. Ketamine is safe when used moderately and at reasonable doses and when not mixed with other medications or alcohol. When combined with alcohol, benzodiazepines, or opioids (to mention a few), ketamine trips can result in death due to the impact on your ability to breathe.

Medically, anesthesiologists use ketamine at much higher doses during surgical procedures than is recommended for mood dosing. Ketamine affects your ability to feel or move your body. Some have inappropriately ingested ketamine and placed themselves in compromising situations, such as using a hot tub, and died. Use caution because abusing ketamine in large amounts, mixed with other substances, or in the wrong setting can be deadly.

Another factor in the "use ketamine with caution" statement is that ketamine addiction is possible. It is not common, but there are enough cases to prompt us to add this here. Ketamine does not build a tolerance and can be used repeatedly without diminished effects. We DO NOT recommend abusing ketamine like this. Ketamine is medicine and makes a pretty poor recreational drug, in our opinion.

One last bit of information: heavy users of ketamine develop cystitis of the bladder, called Ketamine Bladder Syndrome. This condition is a permanent and debilitating syndrome impacting your bladder and urinary function. This risk is yet another reason to avoid regular ketamine use. Our use of ketamine was time-limited and focused on reducing our depression and anxiety symptoms during a tough time in life.

Medication/Drug Interactions:

Cannabis- Cannabis has a strong and unpredictable synergy with the psychedelic effects of ketamine, resulting in increased visual hallucinations, confusion, disorientation, and increased nausea.

Alcohol/Benzodiazepines/Opioids- We grouped these because they are all VERY dangerous to combine with ketamine. It would be best if you avoided all respiratory depressant medications or substances (i.e., downers) with ketamine because they can cause severe impairment of respirations, which can lead to death.

Les's Story

I will start by reiterating the same thing we have hammered home throughout this chapter: Ketamine should not be a recreational thing. It poses a minor risk for addiction and, if abused, can result in permanent damage to your bladder. Thank you, and that concludes our public service announcement.

For me, ketamine was what kept me from losing myself during a traumatic divorce. Once or twice a week, we would take ketamine, and I would have a marked decrease in my depression and anxiety. My research on ketamine has led me to conclude that it is the most potent legal treatment for depression and addiction. I believe that ketamine has the power to help cure, yes cure, some people's depression and to reduce symptoms in most patients.

Ketamine is a weird and wild medicine. The dissociative effects make you feel separate from your body and even time. Mixed with the distinct and powerful psychedelic nature of the medicine at the "K-hole" level, it is an experience like no other. I find it highly visual, with vivid and highly detailed imagery with every trip. It is hard to explain it all, but ketamine feels like I return to the same "world" each time.

Once, I felt I had finally reached the deepest part of the K-hole. I had taken a 200 mg dose intranasally and was feeling the trip intensely, with fast and confusing landscapes zipping past me. Down and down I went, seemingly forever. Suddenly, I landed, which is weird because ketamine trips for me are always moving. This time, I stopped, and what sprouted up around me was the forest glade I had found over a year ago while on psilocybin. Instantly, I knew and felt the Earth Mother with me.

Not one to waste a moment, I asked my new questions, motivated by a calling I felt deep inside. "How do I help others?" She responded, "You must heal yourself before you can heal others." *(What? Ugh.)* I had spent over 18 months healing all kinds of shit. I asked and asked but only ever received the same answer. My time was short, just as it was before, and I left the forest glade and returned slowly to the surface of my mind.

I was confused and left feeling a bit hopeless. I had taken heroic doses of mushrooms, LSD, and tons of MDMA/MDA; what would it take to "heal?" I began to think that I needed something like Ayahuasca to break through. Still, I couldn't deny what the Earth Mother had told me. I didn't feel I had enough to give. I sensed weariness in my soul.

I continued to use ketamine as needed, though less than before, to help manage my symptoms of depression and anxiety, but I was not closer to healing. It wasn't until a friend randomly and surreptitiously invited us to an Iboga retreat that I understood what the Earth Mother told me. In that ceremony, I finally set down my burden and realized I was not broken at all and that my need to "heal" was based on an innate belief that I was grievously damaged. I was already whole, and I needed to believe that. My beliefs about myself have changed, and I haven't touched ketamine since. I don't need it. While exploring the ketamine universe is tempting, I no longer need it. However, I see so many people who still need ketamine, and with the availability of local ketamine clinics this medicine is accessible legally for those who need it.

Home Rolling

Using ketamine at home for therapeutic reasons is very accessible due to the relative safety of ketamine combined with the short duration of intoxication (60 minutes or so). Whether at the psycholytic or psychedelic dosing, due to the impact on your ability to walk safely, you should plan on laying on a bed or couch for the duration of the trip.

We have found that you want your music queued up and your spot in bed ready before you take ketamine because the effects can hit within the first few minutes. A small amount of preparation goes a long way. Also, ketamine's short effect time means you don't have to worry about snacks, drinks, or electrolytes.

Regarding music, we have used our favorite song playlists and dedicated playlists for ketamine therapy. If you use pop songs, the words and beats will direct your ketamine journey significantly. If you choose to use a ketamine or psychedelic therapy playlist, you will find that the music carries you along in your journey but does not cause abrupt shifts or changes in the trip like pop songs can.

Use in Therapy

Ketamine's use in therapy is why this chapter exists. Ketamine, in our opinion, is the most effective legal medicine available in the U.S. for the treatment of depression and suicidal thoughts. When combined with post-treatment integration or therapy, ketamine appears to be able to cure depression in many patients.

Researchers are still examining the evidence for the curative properties of ketamine-assisted psychotherapy (KAP). Still, the hundreds of therapists using KAP across the country are reporting that their clients are free from depression after just a handful of sessions. The word "cure" is not used in mental health, but it is starting to pop up more and more as the use of KAP becomes more prevalent.

Takeaways

Ketamine is a medicine, and we do not recommend it for partying. Given the dissociative anesthetic aspects, ketamine in high doses can be fatal if used in the wrong situation. That said, if someone I knew was struggling with depression or thoughts of suicide, I would hustle them into a ketamine clinic and seek ketamine treatment *immediately*.

Some clinics are already using ketamine for acute suicidal crises, and hopefully, one day, this will be the gold standard of treatment. Clinics and Emergency Departments using ketamine for acutely suicidal patients can administer ketamine (usually IM or IV), and the patient's symptoms stabilize to the point they can be discharged and follow up with mental health professionals on an outpatient basis instead of being held in an acute inpatient psychiatric unit involuntarily.

Ketamine is more effective and faster acting than typical antidepressants (which take 4 to 6 weeks for full effect).

If you're receiving ketamine treatment, be sure to have a playlist! Experiment with songs with and without lyrics. Look for playlists explicitly created for ketamine.

Set an intention, and allow your mind to heal itself.

You must let go and allow your mind to flow with the experience. Refrain from fighting where your mind goes or where the experience takes you, which can result in a challenging trip.

If you can, seek out Ketamine Assisted Psychotherapy (KAP). KAP is much more effective than simply ketamine alone (via any route) and allows you to heal the root causes of your depression instead of just treating the symptoms.

If you prefer a clinic but feel you can't afford the costs, some providers will do sliding scale fees, particularly for Veterans.

We do not recommend ketamine when tripping alone; find a trip sitter at the least, and proceed with caution.

Ketamine is not recommended just for fun, but it can be powerfully healing for both parties in a coupleship if done together.

2C-B: THREE-DROP PROBLEMS

Introduction

2C-B is a novel psychedelic that has unique properties that somewhat resemble MDMA and LSD, though the effects of 2C-B are very unique. There is little research on 2C-B, and it is not currently the subject of intense research. We first heard of 2C-B while watching a documentary on Sasha Shulgin, where Sasha Shulgin's wife, Ann (a lay therapist), described 2C-B as her favorite drug discovered by her husband (a genius chemist) because it was the most fun to have sex on. Anne beautifully stated in their documentary *Dirty Pictures*, "If you can't make love on it, then there's something not quite right." [66] *(Definitely two of our heroes!)*

Another exciting characteristic of 2C-B is the prevalence of "open-eye visuals." Most classic psychedelics, at reasonable doses, don't provide any visual hallucinations with your eyes open, with visions more typical with eyes closed. *(This is highly individual as we have a close friend who has experienced open-eye visuals on very low doses of most substances.)* 2C-B reliably produces these visuals with greater intensity as the dose increases. Beyond 50 mg of 2C-B, the trip's visuals and all other aspects become overwhelming and incredible *(even Byrd realized this once she finished dying during her first 2C-B experience!)*.

While one of the most common of the "novel psychedelics," 2C-B is not easy to obtain in comparison to other classic psychedelics, but it was sure worth it. Our experiences are limited due to the challenges of securing 2C-B, but we will share what we can.

History

We haven't mentioned Alexander "Sasha" Shulgin in this book because we never set out to write a comprehensive history of psychedelics. Others have done this better than we ever could have. Sasha Shulgin is arguably one of the most outstanding chemists in history, with over 200 psychedelic compounds discovered in his lab, including 2C-B. While he didn't discover MDMA, Sasha Shulgin's book *PiHKAL: A Chemical Love Story* described and shared the procedures to synthesize MDMA and many other psychedelics with anyone with an understanding of chemistry. This democratizing of psychedelic production has led to the current abundance of the many psychedelics produced in clandestine labs across the world. [17]

Legal Status

2C-B is illegal and is a Schedule I substance in the US. 2C-B is off the radar as a therapeutic substance, so we can expect it to remain banned for many years to come.

Byrd's Story

Les read various reports online related to 2C-B and dosing. Some claimed liquid 2C-B was fake and, after "drinking a vial," experienced no effects. Others recommended anywhere from 1 to 3 drops as a typical dose. Les located liquid 2C-B, and we used the dropper to administer three drops sublingually on the night of a special occasion. *(This was not supposed to be a Go Big or Go Home near-death moment. It turned out to be *sigh*).*

It didn't taste great, but it wasn't the worst (for example, ketamine tastes worse, LSD not as bad, MDMA is *the worst*), kind of like a chemical alcohol. Surprisingly, the medicine took effect much quicker than expected, and within 5 minutes, the patterns on our boho bed sheet started to swirl and move. I began feeling like I was crawling out of my skin. My nerves were tingling, I started sweating, and I felt my nerves randomly firing all over my body. And then I became nauseous. I have thrown up at least once on every single substance I have ever taken, and it is par for the course for Byrd.

I started throwing up and continued throwing up until my stomach was empty, and then several more dry heaves for good measure. I thought I was dying. We went from planning to have fun to my brain screaming I had made an appalling lapse in judgment. In 5 minutes, we went from celebrating a special occasion with a new fun adventure to crisis and maybe death. I was disoriented, and my mind panicked, thinking, "We have gone to a terrible place now."

I kept thinking my kids were going to find me dead, and I felt bad for telling them psychedelics are fun and healing. At the same time, I was asking Les why people would create something like this. Didn't they want people to come back for more? I thought the point was repeat customers, and we can't repeat if we are dead?!

I had to lay down on the bed and couldn't move. Any movement made me sick. Talking made me sick. I couldn't open my eyes because everything was moving around me, and that made me feel sicker. When I did open my eyes between puking, I could see neon colors in a paisley design on the walls around me. It sounded like I was in a tunnel of fog, and sounds were far away, moving slower than usual and with a strange echo.

2C-B hit every one of my senses, and my brain was completely overwhelmed. I was swirling away somewhere in my mind, and all I could hear was Les's voice talking to me. I thought for sure I was dying. My mind went back and forth between going to the ED and the reaction we would inevitably get. (*Seriously, who thinks it's a good idea to take drugs off strangers on the internet?! Take three, they said; it will be fun, they said. What was I thinking?!*) Later, a facilitator told us that significant changes in your mind require your conscious mind first to be overwhelmed to break through the barriers we naturally erect as we move through everyday life. Repealing the conscious self is part of ego death. I wasn't planning on a spiritual or healing experience. I was planning to have fun. The sudden dissonance added to the intensity.

I started begging God to forgive me for my stupidity. In the back of my mind, I could hear a response, "Uh huh, and in a few months, you will be back here again. You took something else and think you're dying." (*Okay, okay maybe there's a pattern there!*) I kept saying, "I'm sorry" over and over. I felt sorry for everything. I felt intense guilt. I felt sorry for all the mistakes I ever made as a parent, the most recent being telling them psychedelics were positive and healing. I felt guilty for every mistake I had ever made, whether as a partner, a co-worker, a Christian, or in general. I apologized until I realized I was sorry for existing and continued apologizing some more.

In between, Les kept talking to me. I couldn't open my eyes, so all I could hear was his voice, talking to me calmly, calling me back. Occasionally, he would tease me, questioning if I was *really* dying. I would start to laugh, feel immediately ill, roll up in a ball crying, and start apologizing to God again. I said over and over, "Never again." And each time, Les laughed and said, "Yeah, right." I pictured myself dying and God shaking His head at me,

"Seriously? Drugs off strangers on the internet?" It struck me how fleeting and precious life is and how short of time I have.

After I stopped throwing up, I lay on the bed, curled on my side, and tried not to move. I continued to apologize. In my mind, I saw myself dead and apologizing to God for everything that ever happened in my life. I went right back to those intense emotions that motivated me to kill myself in the first place. I had done life all wrong, and I could never fix it. I had messed up, and I couldn't ever fix it. I kept apologizing. Les asked me what I was sorry for and then suddenly said, "Maybe this is good. This sounds like ego death. This could be really good for you." *(It is always helpful to have an empathetic partner when you're dying. *rolling eyes* He's lucky I was too sick to throw something his direction).*

As I kept apologizing, it hit my soul that I could apologize until I died, and it wasn't going to do any good. I wasn't making anything better by apologizing. I was making everything worse and wasting my life feeling regret and self-hatred. These emotions weren't helping anyone, least of all me. I was struck by how much time I had wasted and continued to waste. I wanted to take my own life because I was stuck in this place of self-recrimination, paralyzed in guilt, self-hatred, and doubt, and unable to move forward.

Inside, I felt like I died; my life as I knew it was over. This life I kept apologizing for was over. I apologized until I died, and now it is over. I comprehended I couldn't apologize anymore; there wasn't anything more to do than say sorry and move forward. God didn't want me to kill myself. God wasn't honored by me killing myself. I wasn't fulfilling the path God had for me or the Commandments by killing myself. I laid down the burdens on my soul, every last action, thought, or memory that haunted me. All of the things I told myself I should have and could have done better. My life until then was finished.

As the physical sickness wore off, Les kept talking to me. The feelings were coming in waves. I was overwhelmed by panic and feeling terrible physically. Then Les would talk to me, commenting on how great the experience was if you weren't throwing up, saying, "I mean, look at all the pretty colors!" I would drift away, and he would draw me back in. His voice was a lighthouse in the swirling storm, bringing me back. He would make a joke, and I would laugh, then start crying again, then laugh again. I told him I wanted my tombstone to read, "Les made her laugh even when she was dying."

Once I opened my eyes again, it was just the two of us lying on our bed, alone in the world. Everything felt far and distant; we had stepped out of time and space, and it was just the two of us naked in bed talking. I sensed myself far away from the world, looking down on it from above in my mind. We began talking and continued for hours. I felt my soul crack open, raw, and vulnerable, and Les waltzed right in and lay down next to me, laughing, teasing me, and allowing me to talk about all the deepest wounds that remained in my soul.

We covered a decade of therapy in a single night. These areas of my wounded soul that I spent years trying to heal in EMDR, Les came in one night and brought healing. I could trust him deep in my soul like no one else. People I thought I could trust had wounded me, especially men. There were walls around my soul and a feeling that I wasn't worth it. Now, I felt myself die, and Les was there for me the whole time. He stayed with me, talking and laughing with me through it all. I faced Hell, and he was there with me. I realized I could trust him with my deepest self.

In the past, the kids and I were rejected in favor of things like alcohol, rage, selfishness, and addiction. In contrast, Les said I was worth it. I was at my lowest, dying, throwing up, crying all over the place, completely undone. He stayed with me, holding, loving, and talking to me. He valued me. A hole had torn open a couple of decades ago inside of me, a well holding all of my dark emotions. Finally, for the first time, the hole started closing up. Throughout the years, I felt I was closer or farther from the hole inside my soul, at my darkest moments, falling, falling, drowning in the ocean of dark emotions inside. And now, for the first time, the hole started getting smaller, stitched back together piece by piece.

We talked about things I hadn't been able to process in therapy, even though I had tried. Les stepped past all those walls I had built so carefully and sat down inside my heart and soul to talk. I felt so unworthy of his loving me. I am so grateful for a chance to live this life together. For the first time in years, life felt incredibly short. Before, life had stretched out in this unending span of years. I tried to survive a day at a time, always waiting for the other shoe to drop. Now, I was conscious of how short and precious the days were in my life.

We talked about the world at large. I looked around and saw all the war and devastation, the disconnection and hate. I felt the time wasted in these terrible endeavors and was struck by how much good we could do if we laid down our weapons and instead worked together to build and solve problems. I felt so heavily the weight of time already wasted. I sensed there were others like us, others who wanted to bring healing, light, and love to the world. I thought of people and issues I struggle with daily, and it just didn't seem necessary. All of that was still there, but it was a distraction from the primary purpose of healing and helping.

We discussed my need to keep apologizing and my feelings of never measuring up or being good enough. I felt incredibly humbled by how much we don't know. A part of me was indignant at all of the people growing up who insisted they "know what will happen when you die." Deep in my soul, I grasped that we don't *know*; no one does, and if someone says they do, this is an arrogant stab in the dark. All my life, I was told I had to check off these boxes, follow these rules, say this prayer, and I would know what would happen when I die. Having almost died, I was humbled to realize we don't know anything at all. I realized we are powerless in the most significant ways. I don't have control over when I take a breath or every time my heart beats, and life could end at any moment. At the same time, I empathize with the need to feel like one knows what will happen, the need to build a little box in life and stay in it to ensure feelings of eternal security. It's scary not knowing. I found that no matter what, we cast ourselves on God's grace in the end.

As we continued talking, I asked myself what this meant for me. What if I'm wrong? I kept coming back to love. I can live a life of love. I remembered the dissonance involved in love versus protection. I realized I couldn't answer all the questions and scenarios right then. All I could do was choose the most loving, righteous path at every intersection and in every decision. It struck me that all of life boils down to choosing, and each little decision adds up to a general pathway and destiny in life. I decided to choose up; whenever I could move in either direction, I was choosing up. I could focus on Hell and fear, or light and love. I choose light and love. When I could forgive or hold a grudge, love or hate, I choose forgiveness and love. I would weigh every decision and ask myself which was up. This I could do. This life I could live.

The trip lasted a little over 3 hours. By 4 hours post-administration, I couldn't feel any effects left. Nothing was moving, no more cool colors. We watched a movie, and the sound was still distorted, and the actors' faces looked unusual. *(I'm sure I saw a third eye once or twice!)* Sometimes, actions would speed up or slow down incongruently. I felt like I had lived a lifetime, covered decades of healing therapy in one psychedelic session, and only a few hours had passed.

The next time we tried 2C-B, I would only take two drops, spaced apart by at least 30 minutes. *(Yes, God was most definitely rolling His eyes and saying, "Again?!")* Sadly, the effect was very mild. The person we bought the drops from changed the advertisement from "A dose is three drops" to "A dose is 1 to 2 drops; start slowly! This stuff is strong!"

(Right. Now you tell us.) Les, of course, tried 3 drops again, though he spaced his out by 30 minutes and made fun of me for being chicken. *(Uh-huh, I know what having three drop problems is like!)*

A couple of months later, we had a kickback with friends, and a couple of them tried the same 2C-B. The drops had dried up, so we reconstituted them. Whatever happened changed the strength of the drops, and our friends had very mild effects comparatively.

On another occasion, we tried 2C-B in a powder form. We swallowed two capsules each. We experienced distorted senses, such as sounds coming from far away, through a tunnel of fog, and saw pretty neon colors in paisley shapes on the walls. At first, I had a strong feeling of my nerves firing oddly and wanting to come out of my skin. I didn't get nauseous and didn't throw up. We giggled and laughed a lot about nothing and everything. All in all, it wasn't even half as powerful as the three drops. Or maybe that first time was the medicine my soul needed, moving me further down the healing path.

Somehow, I felt like I died that night. I sensed an end to a significant part of my life and a fresh start. I realized wanting to die so badly, I had, in a way, finally reached that death. I laid down many of the previous sorrows and could move forward again. I felt such gratitude for life. Having come so near to dying, back when I was the closest to suicide and now metaphorically, I realize every single day and every breath is a gift. I am grateful.

Thoughts from EMDR: November 2023

We went back in time to one of the most traumatic nights of my life.

Processing reprocessing.

After weeks of work, revelation finally hit me. I could no longer see myself in that situation. The Byrd I am now would make different choices, would see the red flags, and wouldn't tolerate abuse even at the lowest level. The Byrd I am now would have left long before we got to that night. The Byrd I am now wouldn't even BE in that situation. I could remember it, but somehow, it was no longer me.

For the first time in many years, I was grateful for who I am now.

I have mourned the loss of innocence, sweetness, naïveté, going with the flow, avoiding conflict, and being liked by everyone. But that version of Byrd couldn't protect herself or her kids. That Byrd believed things that weren't true or healthy. The person I am now is tougher and wiser, struggles with darkness, sees and feels the world's pain, sets boundaries, and sometimes says and does things people don't like. This Byrd is safe and can make better choices for herself and her family.

I accept who I have become while wanting to continue changing for the better.

Love with safety.
Love with boundaries.
Love that says no.
Love that can protect.

Dosages and Effects

Our experience with 2C-B is limited to a handful of experiences, but we will share our expertise with dosing and some effects commonly reported by others.

Onset: 30 to 60 minutes (oral capsules); 1 to 10 minutes (oral 2C-B drops)

Peak: 2 hours

Duration: 4 hours (up to 6 at higher doses)

For simplicity, we will break the dosing of 2C-B into 25 mg intervals.

Low/Medium Dose (25 mg):

25 mg is approachable and should give a solid effect without overly intoxicating.

Mood Effects: You will likely experience enhanced mood and euphoria, increased sociability, and empathy. Some individuals reported anxiety or paranoia.

Visual Effects: You may experience enhanced colors and brightness, light optical patterning, and afterimages with mild geometric overlays with open eyes.

Sensory Effects: You will get enhanced tactile sensations, similar to MDMA. Also, you may experience synesthesia (e.g., seeing sounds or hearing colors), a rad effect we rarely experience.

Physical Body Effects: Like MDMA, you will experience increased body temperature and sweating, nausea or gastrointestinal discomfort, and a mild increase in heart rate and blood pressure. 2C-B can make fine motor skills more jerky, and you may experience an internal feeling of being unsettled or jittery.

Physical Activity: You will enjoy enhanced stamina, energy, and desire to move or dance. You might experience mild coordination difficulties, but nothing you can't handle.

Moderate/High Dose (50 mg):

This dose is approachable, but things ratchet up a few notches. We found this dose extremely "fun," with fits of giggles and laughing throughout the trip. This dose also had no day-after effects, making this a great Sunday afternoon drug.

Mood Effects: You will be experiencing intense euphoria and happiness. Some report equally intense dysphoria. Negative moods have not been our experience; if you are careful with your set and setting, you should be good. Expect significant alterations in perception of reality with the potential for some anxiety or paranoia *(remember to surrender to the experience)*.

Visual Effects: Stronger visual hallucinations, including complex geometric patterns, are possible here. Also, intense alterations in visual perception of the environment can occur. Lights become bright with stars and halos.

Sensory Effects: Tactile sensation will ramp up, though we didn't find 2C-B very sexual at this dose. Sounds are altered, like listening from a distance or through a tunnel. We wouldn't say 2C-B is going to enhance music like LSD does. Synesthesia, when you hear music but see shapes, is also more likely at this dose.

Physical Body Effects: Increases in your body temperature are more significant. This temperature dysregulation could cause hyperthermia if your environment is too hot or you are dehydrated. Some report substantial gastrointestinal discomfort and increased nausea. Heart rate and blood pressure increase further at this dose, which can be risky for those with cardiovascular issues. Not enough is known about 2C-B to say it won't cause cardiac complications at higher doses.

Physical Activity: Heightened energy and a desire to move continues at this dose. Some report significant impairment in engaging in coordinated activities. You won't be assembling Ikea furniture or building a house of cards. That said, essential activities are very doable.

Extreme Dose (75 mg):

Exercise caution at doses greater than 50 mg. We need additional research for high doses, but overdoses of 2C-B have not resulted in permanent injury or death. Use at your own risk. This dose will act more like LSD in the greater-than 500 microgram dosing, which means you can expect very psychedelic and earth-shattering symptoms.

We presume the sketchy "three-drop problems" resulted from this dose. Byrd's story highlights the significant psychedelic effects of high-dose 2C-B, with her ego death as evidence. Les found this dose of 2C-B highly enjoyable and psychedelic, with the walls wobbling, open-eye visuals, and an extreme feeling of euphoria and connection.

Mood Effects: Anything is possible but count on it being extreme (euphoria or dysphoria). Total disconnection from reality is very likely and will require you to practice your surrender skills.

Visual Effects: Overwhelming visual hallucinations that can dominate your perceived world will happen. Lean into it because it is beautiful. You may experience a complete alteration or loss of visual connection with reality.

Sensory Effects: Your reality will be profoundly altered, making sensory effects hard to describe. Changes in your sensory perception are potentially extreme and may cause some distress. You will likely feel some intense synesthesia that can add to the loss of connection with reality.

Physical Body Effects: Severe increases in body temperature are possible, so keep your physical environment cool. There is a high risk of severe nausea and vomiting, especially if you are susceptible to nausea and vomiting when using psychedelics. Also, an unknown higher increase in heart rate and blood pressure can pose a potential health risk to those with cardiac issues. Use caution and consult with your physician if you have concerns.

Physical Activity: Again, we are in the Wild West of psychedelics, and the potential for extreme energy or, conversely, significant lethargy is possible. Expect substantial impairment in motor skills and coordination. No acrobatics for you. The only thing keeping you from being pulled into yourself, as happens at high doses of psilocybin and LSD, is the intense feeling of connection and the open-eye sensory overload.

Risk, Safety, and Addiction

2C-B is understudied, and not much is known with great certainty. In the rare reports of overdoses of 2C-B, individuals did not die or suffer from lasting adverse effects. Also, in the few cases of overdose, individuals were hospitalized for hyperthermia primarily. [16]

As a very potent psychedelic, especially at high doses, the psychological impact of an overdose is not to be underestimated. We urge caution with 2C-B, especially in doses exceeding 50 mg.

The addiction profile of 2C-B is not known, but in our extensive research, no cases of 2C-B addiction were found. You can abuse 2C-B, like every other substance, but it does not have a chemical hook that causes withdrawals or cravings.

Overall, 2C-B seems relatively safe for occasional use at reasonable doses. Sasha Shulgin reported taking 100 mg of 2C-B with no ill effects as a result. [17]

Medication/Drug Interactions:

With little information available on 2C-B, we will include the interactions listed on PsychonautWiki (a surprisingly good source of information). [39]

Cannabis- As with all psychedelics, cannabis has a strong and unpredictable synergy with psychedelics. As a force multiplier, remember that not only will the "positive" effects of the psychedelic be heightened. If combined, use much smaller doses of both substances and go slow.

Amphetamines/Cocaine- While limited *(read: no)* research on 2C-B exists, we can extrapolate some risks. All psychedelics become dangerous when mixed with amphetamines and cocaine. These are addictive and can cause Serotonin Syndrome.

Lithium- As a common psychiatric medication, Lithium has been reported to increase the risk of seizures and psychosis. Combining Lithium with any psychedelic is strongly discouraged!

Tramadol- This is a prescription pain medication. Tramadol reduces the seizure threshold when combined with serotonergic drugs (e.g., all psychedelics) and also increases the risk for Serotonin Syndrome. [40]

Les's Story

I had very high hopes for 2C-B, but the hype hasn't quite matched our experiences. That is not to say that 2C-B has no place in our lives, but it doesn't bring enough to the table to be anything but a novel drug for those nights when "something different" is desired.

As you read in Byrd's story, we started with a heroic dose of 2C-B. I don't regret this; it was beautiful, and the connection was beyond anything we had encountered. Stepping into her soul and comforting her as she died over and over again was something unique you don't get to experience often in life. That first experience was the only one where I could understand how people like 2C-B for sex. After the ego dissolution, we attempted to make love on the backside of the peak. The synesthesia and sensations were so intense we weren't sure if we enjoyed it. Well, I enjoyed it, but I am not sure I can handle that intensity of sexual stimulation for very long or even very often.

At lower doses (25 mg and 50 mg), 2C-B has not impressed us much. The open-eye visuals are engaging, but the distortion of your visual perception makes the world seem too weird at times. For example, sitting in a hotel room in Cancun, we took 50 mg of 2C-B after coming down from MDMA, and Byrd pointed out the floor-to-ceiling mirror in the front hallway. Wow! It looked like there was a whole other room there. We knew it was the mirror, but our brains couldn't understand what we saw. It seems minor, but everything just looked wrong, like it shouldn't be that way, but you can't figure out what is wrong. *(Most disconcerting, your partner's face can be distorted too!)*

The one reason I will keep 2C-B around is because when mixed with psilocybin, movies are awesome. I took two grams of psilocybin and 25 mg of 2C-B and watched a sci-fi movie. What an experience! At the movie's midpoint, the graphics became intensely vivid and sometimes seemed to extend from the screen like a 3-D movie. This movie was over ten years old, so I know the special effects weren't as significant as I experienced. 2C-B is a trip I will undoubtedly repeat.

Overall, 2C-B is a novelty experience and unlikely to provide more than a fun and odd night for you and your partner. Given the chance, it might find a niche in your drug box.

Home Rolling

Treat 2C-B like MDMA, MDA, and LSD. Ensure that you remain hydrated, your environment isn't crazy hot or sun-exposed, you are comfortable chilling for 4 to 6 hours, and you have addressed your 3 S's (set, setting, and surrender). Otherwise, start low and work your way up.

Use in Therapy

Officially, we haven't heard a lot of talk about using 2C-B in therapy, but we assume that some underground therapists are using it due to the properties of 2C-B at lower doses.

Takeaways

Start slowly and ease your way into it, gradually increasing the dose. If you're sensitive, consider fasting at least 4 hours before an experience, especially if it's the first time using something.

Even a challenging trip can be incredibly healing. Sometimes, it's healthy for the mind to feel out of control and to reach the end of yourself.

Test anything you self-administer! You don't want to be wondering if what you just took contained fentanyl, especially if you start throwing up. *(But what would we know?)*

CANDY FLIPPING: HOW TO MAKE YOUR TRIP LAST FOR 24 HOURS

Introduction

Mixing any substance with another substance is often referred to as polysubstance or multi-substance use. The street term for mixing psychedelics is "flipping." Online, there are innumerable recipes for mixing substances. Some of these are not advised, and some are downright dangerous.

We stay away from substances with high addiction potential, except alcohol, which we drink in moderation and do not typically mix with psychedelics. Having worked in mental health and rehab and given personal life experiences, neither of us wants to risk addiction. In addition, adding one substance to another always increases risk because it's more of everything and more difficult for your body to process.

That said, some psychedelic substances can be safely mixed for enhanced or more prolonged effects. Flipping is a more advanced level of psychedelic experience, and you want to start slow and ease into it should you choose to experiment in this direction. Do your research before actually experimenting, as there are many points of view as to what order to self-administer each substance, recommended dose, etc.

Candy Flipping

The term Candy Flipping refers to mixing LSD and MDMA specifically. A study in 1998 confirmed that MDMA and LSD taken together have a synergistic effect, producing a "maximal MDMA-like experience."[47] In 2023, researchers conducted a double-blind, randomized, placebo-controlled study with 24 participants comparing the effects of MDMA and LSD taken alone and MDMA combined with LSD. The effects of the MDMA and LSD taken together lasted longer, with higher blood plasma concentrations of the LSD compared with either substance administered alone. Researchers also found MDMA and LSD dispensed jointly resulted in a longer time for the body to process the substances compared with either substance independently, also known as a longer half-life. [46] Basically, LSD and MDMA together make the effects of each substance more intense, and the experience lasts longer.

During early experimentation, we realized 100 mcg of LSD combined with 1 MDA would last an entire night and into the following day, leaving us alert and unexpectedly refreshed after missing a night of sleep. As we continued to try different combinations, we were able to extend a candy flipping session to 24 hours by taking 300 mcg of LSD, and after this peaked, self-administering 3 points of MDMA. We typically take the LSD, and then approximately 4 hours later take the MDMA.

One thing we like about Candy Flipping is it allows for time spent with friends and then time spent alone as a couple. Over and over, when we were exploring just the two of us, we felt a strong motivation to share what we had found with others. We especially wanted to reach out to those closest to us. We enjoy hanging out in small groups with tight-knit friends, enhanced with mushrooms or LSD, laughing and talking for hours over a campfire in the forest or at someone's house with snacks. Then, after our friends were ready to head home, we split off to be alone as a couple, taking MDMA and enjoying our time just the two of us. *(We tease our friends that they don't want to be around us for this part anyway!)* As weekends with friends are rare and constantly compete with our weekends set aside just for the two of us, we can enjoy the best of both worlds. We are incredibly blessed to have friends who are willing to explore psychedelics, and all of us have found various manners of healing and connection through psychedelic substances, even while hanging out as a group.

Nexus Flipping

The Nexus Flip is 2C-B combined with MDMA, also known as the Honey Flip. Typically, people self-administer MDMA first and then take 2C-B after the peak. We recently tried out the Nexus Flip and found that it was smoother than just 2C-B alone (e.g., less shaky muscles), and the visuals were more pronounced than we have experienced before while Ali Flipping or taking just 2C-B.

Ali Flipping

The Ali Flip is a combination of LSD, MDMA, and 2C-B. Online, we read that some take LSD, followed by MDMA after the LSD peaks, and then 2C-B after the MDMA peaks. This mix is also known as a combination of a Candy Flip and a Nexus Flip. We tried this once, and while the LSD and MDMA combo was as stunning as usual, we didn't notice any effect from the 2C-B other than some pretty visual colors.

Hippie Flipping

The Hippie Flip is a combination of MDMA and shrooms. We haven't tried this combo yet, but we plan to. Some relate that mixing these two substances decreases the dark or sad feelings that can arise with higher doses of mushrooms. One wit on Reddit shared that by taking MDMA with your shrooms, "You stare into the abyss, and the abyss smiles back." Given Byrd's previous challenging trips on mushrooms, we have considered adding a dose of MDMA to lighten the experience of enlightenment.

Jedi Flipping

The Jedi Flip is a combination of LSD, MDMA, and shrooms. We haven't tried this combo yet. Some try this out of sheer curiosity, others to achieve a deeper exploration of consciousness. Jedi Flipping is said to produce a euphoric psychedelic experience. [61] MDMA is overwhelmingly positive, while LSD and shrooms are known for producing visuals. Taken together, these can inspire a profoundly spiritual experience. The dose of each substance self-administered will alter your experience.

We love the feeling of stealing a night. We can work all day, stay up all night *and* the following day, sleep the next night, and get back on track with our schedule with two days of the weekend left. What's not to love? This scheduling method ensures all substances are entirely out of our system before returning to work, as we take our professional roles very seriously.

With any flipping, if you take lower doses, you can usually repeat the experience sooner. If you take higher doses, it will take longer for the neurotransmitters to reset, so you will have to wait longer between experiences. Once, we tried Candy Flipping two nights in a row. We wanted to test the claim that these drugs are self-limiting. The second night, we felt nothing. Maybe a little bit more alertness, but nothing else.

Another time, we self-administered LSD alone two weekends in a row and noticed the second time had a drastically reduced effect. Honestly, the inability to take psychedelics back to back is a relief. No matter how much fun or good we feel, we must break between experiences.

We found marijuana to be very helpful in easing the comedown after any substance such as LSD, MDA, or MDMA. For this purpose, self-administer marijuana long after the peak of anything else is past. Marijuana used during or immediately after the peak of another substance potentiates other substances, often enhancing the effects or making the effects last longer.

Marijuana potentiation is robust when Candy Flipping. With LSD and MDMA combined, we might be up for 24 hours after we take the LSD. When ready to go to bed, we are deliriously tired and sometimes have trouble tracking a conversation or movie but don't feel ready to fall asleep. Byrd sometimes starts to feel sad as the effects are waning, if for no other reason than because the incredible experience is over. Smoking some pot enhances the desire to sleep and eases the comedown, including any sad emotions. Walking outside can also help reduce melancholy emotions during the ending phase. You can also cuddle naked and watch a movie together.

Byrd's Story

As we grew more comfortable with substances, we slowly explored mixing different things to find our favorite outcomes. So far, our favorite is 300 mcg of LSD, followed by 3 MDMA (or 1 MDA and 2 MDMA).

The first time we tried mixing LSD with MDA, we were on the beach in Mexico. It was epic! We hung out on the beach all night, skinny dipping, talking, swimming in and out of the waves, admiring the stars. The night sky looks incredible with this combination! The trip lasts all night long. Of course, we could try this during the day, but we adore looking at the stars, and it's too bright to be outside when our pupils are enlarged.

On another trip camping in the forest, we tried 200 mcg of LSD and 3 MDMA on a warm, clear summer evening. We camped on the edge of a lookout, admiring the setting sun as the light faded. That night, we had some challenging real-world topics to sort through. I was considering applying for a higher leadership position in another department; however, I left that department a few years earlier to decrease stress.

Les and I took time that night to sort through what I wanted. How did I want my life to look going forward? What did I love doing as a nurse? What brought value to my life? When I was older, what would I regret, and what would I remember fondly? Finally, what was the best decision for my physical and mental health? I looked at my health and felt it wasn't worth compromising for work. In the end, I realized what I truly wanted to do was work with psychedelics. For the first time since working with pregnant teens, I found I was genuinely passionate about an area of nursing. I could see so much potential for helping others with the breakthroughs in research and the re-emergence of using psychedelics as healing medicine. Instead of pursuing higher leadership, I decided to look for an opportunity to pursue the use of psychedelics in nursing.

As the sun rose, I was amazed to see the hillside breathing. The whole cliffside was moving as if breathing in and out. The rocks at our feet were respiring, and when we touched the stones, there was movement in response, almost as if the hard rock was a spongy material. It was incredible to see the whole world alive in a new way, from each rock and tree to the entire hillside. It reminded me of the belief that there is life and spirit in everything around us, including inanimate objects. While the effect wore off, I will never look at the natural world around me the same.

One of my all-time favorite memories was the night we drove to the Grand Canyon and took an LSD & MDA combo. We arrived at the canyon at about 9 p.m., took the LSD, and hiked to my favorite outlook from the top of the canyon. Once settled at the outlook, we self-administered the MDA. We spent the rest of the night looking at all the stars, talking, and making love. The top was mildly temperate, but a warm breeze blew up to the top of the canyon walls, making the night deliciously warm.

The North Rim of the Grand Canyon has been identified as one of the darkest skies in the U.S. and, thus, amazing for watching stars. Every time we kept thinking we should head back, we were captivated all over by the beauty of the sky spread out all around us. We watched Shooting Stars all night. The sky slowly started to lighten as the canyon walls' sharp edges took shape and then gradually changed to pale rose pink. Eventually, we caught the first rays of the sunrise shooting across the edge of the vast canyon below.

We watched until the sun rose over the canyon walls, then hiked back to our car. It was an unforgettable night.

Another of my favorite memories was a time we experienced up at our property. When I was at my lowest, struggling the most with depression, I purchased property in the forest. Working with my therapist, I identified how much living in the forest meant to my soul. Les was renting a cabin in the area at the time. *(The same cabin where we tried mushrooms for the first time years ago.)* After exploring the area, we wanted to purchase a property. Hands down, it is my favorite part of the forest, with many different kinds of evergreens, dense underbrush, and a wide assortment of plants and animals. As an additional bonus, my favorite trail to run in the mountains starts 2 miles away!

We looked up vacant property parcels on the county website. I wrote letters to 5 landowners, introducing myself as a native of the area and inquiring if they were interested in selling. Two of the owners responded, offering to sell. *(What??? How did that even work?!)* I purchased just over an acre of beautiful forest, dreaming of putting a tiny home on the property. On days when I felt the most down, I could go outside in the forest and remember my dream, finding a reason to take another step forward and live another day.

After purchasing, I found out that the access to the property was complicated and received quotes upwards of $100,000 to install a driveway from the road above. We met with each of the neighbors around us, and eventually, everyone agreed for us to access the property using the dirt road another neighbor owned. There were more setbacks with developing a tiny home (unexpected regulations and costs, etc.), so Les designed a tiny home with enough room for all of us but remaining under 600 square feet.

One fall afternoon, we drove to the mountains looking for pretty fall foliage. Sometimes, I struggle with escalating feelings of depression and sadness as the weather turns colder and the days shorten. Holidays combined with cold and darkness can pose a tough adjustment. We hoped finding colorful fall foliage would put a happier spin on the changing seasons. Unfortunately, we were largely unsuccessful. We drove back to town, and I fought the darkness inside, pushing back against the creeping waves.

The following weekend, we had a campfire with friends at our property. We were shocked to find the gorgeous fall we had been looking for all over the state in our new backyard! Brilliant reds, oranges, yellows, and a carpet of falling leaves! We enjoyed a psychedelic-enhanced campfire with friends and then split off to camp alone as a couple.

We stayed up all night with an LSD and MDMA combo. It was beyond words beautiful. Our lives circled back, once again living in the forest, this time on our property, feeling incredible healing, connection, love, and happiness. The towering pines swayed, a testament to hundreds of years; come what may, they are still standing. The oak bushes were unfailingly flexible, bending and bowing to storms but springing back fresh and green every spring. As the sun started rising, we saw a mating pair of hawks circling around and around in the crown of trees above us.

It was such an incredible realization to know we were home and together. We are healing a little more each day. We are committed to each other and dedicated to reaching out to those around us in restoration and love.

Thoughts from EMDR: November 2023

No one is coming to save me.

My whole life, I looked up to people who were older and wiser. When I got older, it would all make sense. Right? When I realized I wouldn't have it figured out, no matter how old I was, I looked more to those around me. Yet the older I get, the more I realize nobody has it figured out. (And the people who think they do are even worse).

I remember all the times my grandmother said, "I don't know, Byrd," and reminded me things work out in time. She had such a different perspective on time, looking back after 70 years. I wish every day she was still here to talk to, even if she didn't have it figured out either. She would have loved to hear all about this stage of my life. We finally got to the good part!

One thing that has hit me lately is I want to do it differently for my kids. I want to leave them with a family that pursues healing, individually and collectively. I refuse to continue passing down unhealthy practices. I want to show them life can, and should be, lived in brutal honesty tied to extraordinary love—no more decades of secrets. No more pretending we have it all together.

We are all trying our best to figure it out, one day at a time. The best gift we can give each other is love, connection, and compassion, a safe place to share openly and laugh at our mistakes while we try to do better in the future.

Risk, Safety, and Addiction

Whenever mixing drugs, you must consider the safety profile of each. Researchers rarely study mixed substances. You must do independent research, combing through Erowid and Reddit for user experiences and dosing recommendations. Flipping is an advanced psychedelic skill and requires a firm understanding of both substances you are combining. If you don't understand how LSD affects you and you mix it with MDA, you will have a potentially wild and unpredictable experience.

It would be best if you always considered the effects of any substance in combination with prescription medications you may be taking. For instance, some people report experiencing symptoms of serotonin cramping when taking an antidepressant and then taking a psychedelic. The psychedelics most impacting serotonin receptors include psilocybin, DMT, mescaline, and LSD. [62]

Go slow, do some research, and don't attempt it if you are new to psychedelics. Flipping can be incredible when done right. Some of our best and most connected experiences have occurred while flipping. Be safe.

Les's Story

Flipping is a blast. As an alchemist at heart, I am always scheming up new ways to combine psychedelics. When I mixed 2C-B with psilocybin, I didn't know what would happen, nor did I have any trip reports to go off of *(but isn't that part of the fun?)*. I believed it was a safe flip, so I tried it out at a reasonable dose. New substances or mixes of drugs are like hiking a new trail for the first time; you never know what you will find, and that adds to the excitement. Psychedelics are an adventure you can enjoy from the comforts of home.

Mixing substances with nuanced or pronounced differences always results in varied and unique experiences. Some drugs are more dominant when combined, with others taking a backseat and adding their flavor to the chief substance. LSD, referred to as the Captain by a friend, is a very dominant substance when mixed with anything else. We haven't tried all possible combinations, but our experience has been that the effects of LSD will be prevalent no matter what substance you add to it.

If you Candy Flip, with both LSD and MDMA taken at the same time, you will find that the MDMA peak is less high, but the duration of that peak can extend by a couple of hours. Acid is excellent for boosting the effects of another substance, so long as you don't mind losing some of the peakiness of the other.

If you look up flipping, you won't find a lot of references to cannabis and psychedelics. The rule of thumb with cannabis and psychedelics is that the cannabis will potentiate or strengthen the effects of all psychedelics. Cannabis particularly potentiates more visual psychedelics like LSD, mushrooms, or ketamine. If mixing with cannabis, be careful, as you need much less of both to reach the same level you would get without cannabis. *(Again, we recommend caution and do not recommend mixing ketamine with any other substances).*

Like with any adventure with psychedelics, learn from our mistakes and start slow and low.

Takeaways

Save your money! Enjoy one experience and wait at least another week before attempting another. Even once a week will be too often if you're doing higher doses, such as three points of MDMA. Lower doses can be repeated more closely, with higher doses requiring a more extended cooling-off period.

Be careful! Start slowly and experiment with caution. Listen to your body and emotions and be mindful of your partner's needs.

Find a partner or friend to enjoy these intimate experiences. Connection doesn't have to be sexual, and one can find healing in platonic relationships as well. *(Though we have a blast experiencing sexual adventures together, just the two of us!)*

There is no one path to healing. Everyone's trail will look a little different. Don't give up yet. Die with psychedelics before dying for real. There are so many options available for healing.

Healing can be fun. *(No, really, it can!)* It's hard work and requires dedication to doing life differently, but it can also be genuinely delightful and eventful. We have found psychedelics allow you to step outside your comfort zone, experience life in a whole new way, and challenge your inner world and preconceived beliefs. It makes sense we call it a trip.

Test, test, test: Fentanyl is serious, and you don't want to take something that's contaminated.

Go outside. <3

IBOGA: YOU ARE ALREADY WHOLE

Introduction

Iboga, Ayahuasca, Peyote, and innumerable other substances are plant-based medicines with psychedelic properties. These plants are part of cultural traditions, handed down for thousands of years in a long line of ancestral knowledge. In fact, mushrooms were also used in ritual ceremonies in Indigenous cultures before gaining popularity in the US. Anne Shulgin stated, "Just about every country and every culture on earth has at least one visionary plant that they use for altering consciousness." [86] Plant medicines are practical, powerful, and for healing rather than fun. These medicines should only be taken as part of a ceremony and with trained guides.

We had the opportunity to participate in an Iboga ceremony facilitated by a member of the Bwiti tribe. The facilitator told us the odds of experiencing Iboga are fewer than winning the Powerball lottery---twice. National Geographic estimates that only 3,000 people outside of Africa had taken Iboga as of 2006. [30] Currently, that estimate has grown to between 10,000 and 40,000 people worldwide. [30] We are honored to share this incredible healing experience.

History

Ayahuasca originates in the Amazon and has been used traditionally in Ecuador, Columbia, Peru, and Brazil. Indigenous people brew Ayahuasca with a combination of 2 types of plants, typically *Banisteriopsis caapi* (B. caapi) vines and leaves from a shrub called chacruna (*Psychotria viridis*), and use the medicine to treat physical ailments and mental problems, and address spiritual crises and social issues. [31] Many people travel to the Amazon to participate in Ayahuasca rituals. Some churches have incorporated the use of Ayahuasca as part of their spiritual traditions.

Dimethyltryptamine (DMT) is one of the main ingredients of Ayahuasca, in conjunction with other psychoactive substances, including the β-carboline derivative alkaloid harmine, harmaline, and tetrahydroharmine. [32] An Ayahuasca trip lasts approximately 4 hours, with participants sharing experiences of first dying or facing their innermost fear, followed by beautiful scenery, spiritual beings, and intellectual and spiritual insights. People describe joy and experiencing a more meaningful life after using Ayahuasca. [32]

A study in 1996 and another in 2008 found that long-term use of Ayahuasca resulted in positive behavioral and lifestyle changes, including relief from addiction. [32] Another study in 2005 found increased joy of life and assertiveness in church members using Ayahuasca. [32] A survey of teens found decreased anxiety and increased optimism, self-confidence, and emotional maturity in those using Ayahuasca compared with their peers. [32] The research supporting the use of Ayahuasca to treat addiction continues to grow, and currently, treatment centers are offering Ayahuasca combined with psychotherapy to treat addiction. A friend recently invited us to participate in an Ayahuasca ceremony. We likely will in the future, but we have not as of yet.

Peyote comes from a small, spineless cactus in Mexico and the American southwest. The main psychoactive ingredient is mescaline. Peyote is eaten or drunk as a tea and has been used in Native American rituals as far back as 5700 years ago. [33] Peyote is very slow growing, taking up to 30 years to grow from seedling to blooming flowers. When harvesters use poor techniques, the whole plant dies. [33] Mescaline has low lipid solubility; thus, only low amounts cross the blood-brain barrier. One study found LSD to be 2000 times more potent as a hallucinogen in producing an altered state of consciousness compared with mescaline. [33] The peak of mescaline lasts approximately 2 hours, and the effects are entirely gone after 10 to 12 hours. [33] Peyote alters the sense of time and distorts perception of the senses, including light, sound, and touch. Participants often report a feeling of being able to communicate with God or other deities and transcend to another space or world. [33]

Native Americans use Peyote to treat pain, fever, skin diseases, autoimmune disorders, and addiction. [33] In addition, studies in 1974 and again in 2005 found mescaline had a therapeutic effect in reducing addiction, with 87% of 452 study participants affected positively. [34] Research on the therapeutic value of mescaline continues.

Iboga comes from the root of the *Tabernanthe iboga* shrubs in Africa. Charcoal cave drawings discovered in a cave in Gabon indicate Indigenous people have been using Iboga for over 2000 years. [30] There are thousands of years of ritual involved in an Iboga ceremony. Each tradition has an origin story, with one familiar tale describing Pygmies watching animals eat the Iboga roots and, from there, learning the psychedelic potential. The Pygmies shared the Iboga tradition with the Bantu people, who comprise the majority of Gabon's population today. [30] As Ibgoa traditions branched out, the Fang tradition combined Christianity and Iboga ceremonial rituals. [35] Each ceremony thanks ancestors who have come before, sharing their knowledge and practices.

As early as 1901, scientists in France and Switzerland isolated the active ingredient Ibogaine from Iboga and began experimenting with its medicinal properties. [30] In the 1960s, psychiatrists in Chile and the United States began using Ibogaine as a therapeutic agent in the mental health field. [30] In 1961, a man from New York, Howard Lotsof, discovered Ibogaine relieved his cravings for heroin without any withdrawal symptoms. [30] To this day, Iboga and Ibogaine are used to effectively treat addiction and withdrawal, particularly for heroin and cocaine. Given legal concerns, medical tourists travel to other countries, such as Mexico, to seek treatment for addiction, anxiety, PTSD, depression, TBI, and other mental health concerns in Ibogaine clinics.

In 2020, a study was conducted in which 51 U.S. Special Forces operatives suffering from PTSD and various mental health and cognitive concerns were given Ibogaine at a clinic in Mexico. [36] The statistically significant results found substantial reductions in suicidal ideation, cognitive impairment, symptoms of PTSD, depression, and anxiety. [36] Participants also had significantly increased psychological flexibility. *(Cheers for neuroplasticity!)* A majority of the Veterans rated the experience as one of the top 5 most personally meaningful (84%), spiritually significant (88%), and psychologically insightful (86%) experiences of their lives. [36]

Stanford University published findings from a study on January 5, 2024, demonstrating the benefits of Ibogaine for Veterans suffering from PTSD. Facilitators gave U.S. Special Forces Veterans suffering from TBI and clinically severe psychiatric symptoms and functional disabilities Ibogaine combined with magnesium at a clinic in Mexico. [37] Of the 30 Veterans, 19 struggled with suicidal ideation, seven had attempted suicide, 23 were diagnosed with PTSD, 14 with anxiety, and 15 had alcohol use disorder. The Veterans described a willingness to try anything to get better. [37] After treatment with Ibogaine, the Veterans reported clinically significant decreases in symptoms of PTSD, depression, and anxiety, with improved cognitive function. These effects persisted for 30 days after treatment when data tracking for the study ended. [37] The authors of the survey are planning to release brain scans showing the benefit of Ibogaine to treat TBI and want to do further research into the use of Ibogaine to heal various neuropsychiatric disorders. [37]

Legal Status

The separate plant components of Ayahuasca are legal; however, once the ingredients are combined, Ayahuasca is formed, which is illegal in every state. Ayahuasca contains DMT, which was one of the substances listed in the Controlled Substances Act in 1970. [31] DMT is a Schedule I substance, and people have been prosecuted for possession of Ayahuasca as recently as 2018. [38] *(No, the government doesn't want anyone having any fun. Pretty sure they thought of everything in 1970).*

Peyote was one of many hallucinogens, such as LSD and psilocybin, used extensively in psychiatry until the UN Convention on Drugs categorized these substances as Schedule I narcotics in 1967. [33] In 1994, the American Indian Religious Freedom Act permitted Peyote harvesting, possession, and consumption only for "bona fide religious ceremon ies."[34] Currently, the Native American Church legally uses Peyote as part of its ritual practices. [33]

Unfortunately, Iboga was one of the psychoactive substances targeted when the War on Drugs kicked off in 1970. The U.S. banned the use, and almost all studies of Ibogaine under the Controlled Substances Act, and many other Western and European countries followed suit. [30] Every year, thousands of Western tourists travel to Mexico, Brazil, Costa Rica, Columbia, and South Africa to participate in medical tourism related to Iboga. A single session can range from $5000 to $15,000. [35]

In the past decade, Gabon has developed a permit system for exporting Iboga. New legislation requires those purchasing or shipping Iboga to meet specific benefits-sharing and environmental requirements. [30] Many groups are working to develop fair trade arrangements in which Indigenous people receive benefits from any Iboga sales, such as new infrastructure, electricity, and clean water. [30] For example, the facilitators of the ceremony we participated in gave the proceeds to a nonprofit developing an ecological retreat for Iboga trees and bringing a village in Gabon clean drinking water.

Byrd's Story

Honestly, no one can describe an Iboga experience accurately. One facilitator said, "It's like describing the color red to a blind man. You have to experience it for yourself." Because the medicine is psychedelic, every journey is unique to each person. I saw nothing psychedelic, no visuals, or even colors or lights behind my eyelids. And yet, the effects were life changing.

Each Iboga treatment involves at least five nights and two separate administrations of the medication. Before participating, we had to undergo a rigorous medical screening and EKG, and a medical team reviewed the results. Iboga causes the pulse and blood pressure to decrease and the QT interval to increase. These effects are minor in a healthy individual but could cause complications in people with certain pre-existing conditions, such as those with arrhythmias, congenital heart defects, or heart murmurs. In addition, we completed a week-long liver cleanse. Facilitators recommend against most medications while taking Iboga, and I weaned off my antidepressant before the ceremony. Most deaths related to Iboga were due to the mismanagement of benzodiazepines while taking Iboga or the use of heroin afterward when the person is no longer tolerant to drugs and the neurotransmitters have been reset.

Iboga is a stimulant, and after receiving the medication on the first and fourth nights, you are often up the entire night and the following day. After each administration, most people are up for 48 hours and only sleep the second night after receiving the medicine. Facilitators administer Ibgoa as part of a significant ceremony, giving each participant ground-up root bark, which is chewed and swallowed. The facilitator works with each participant to determine the appropriate dose based on each person's unique needs. Every day, we participated in guided meditation, and one of the days, we enjoyed a breathtaking sound bath.

Before beginning, we each took time to state our intentions. We shared these statements with the group while sitting around a campfire, speaking as if our intentions had already happened. I thought briefly about my hopes and purposes for participating in the ceremony. With heartfelt honesty, I hesitantly declared, "I love and forgive myself. My soul is at peace." I had no idea how true these words would become or the trial of the soul required before attaining these intentions.

The facilitators describe the first night as the medicine purging the brain and body of anything that needs to be healed. We were given the medicine and laid on mats in the dark with eye masks and Bwiti music playing. While I didn't experience anything truly psychedelic, my mind was flooded with thoughts all night long. My thoughts weren't racing, but they came one after the other. At first, I thought maybe the medicine wasn't working; the effects were that minimal. My brain screamed this was boring, and I couldn't possibly lay there with my thoughts all night. I longed for a distraction. I realized I was so uncomfortable being with myself, my thoughts, and all the emotions going on that my mind would generate the sensation of being "bored," and then I would find a way to distract myself. It was a method of my mind protecting itself. I can't remember ever being alone with myself and my thoughts to this extent.

When I first felt the medicine kicking in, I had a feeling like I was on a raft going down a river, spinning, and my pulse started racing. I tried to let go and flow with the sensations, expecting the Iboga to overwhelm my senses, but my fight or flight kicked in, and I internally panicked. Immediately, almost 80% of the symptoms disappeared. I felt like I hadn't taken anything at all. After a little while, I received more Iboga. This time, the feeling of floating and spinning came and went, but it was never overpowering. The medicine causes the eyes to move rapidly from side to side, similar to the effects of bilateral stimulation prompted during EMDR or the rapid eye movements during REM sleep. I knew if I sat up, I would throw up. I alternated from feeling nauseous to feeling nothing throughout the night. My mind settled into what felt like the beginning stages of sleep while also very awake. The best way to describe this state is "awake dreaming" or "waking sleep."

As the night progressed, my thoughts took a very negative and even paranoid tone. At one point, I thought, "Oh my gosh, if this is what is going on in my head all the time, this is a very dark place! No wonder I'm depressed." I honestly had no idea all those thoughts were constantly under the surface and how much energy I was spending to fight them off day in and day out. Our facilitator explained, "Iboga gives a microphone to your thoughts, so all of the things you're thinking are amplified, and you can hear them clearly. You can't ignore them."

All night long, I fought off negative thoughts. It felt so different from my usual thoughts that I couldn't believe all that negativity was coming from inside me. At one point, my thoughts about Les started taking me down a rabbit hole. At first, I argued with myself, but then I saw his face in my mind and thought, "Stop! I know who Les is!" The rest of the night, I had no more doubts about us.

When we started the session, the facilitators said they don't usually let couples journey together. Traditionally, facilitators move couples to opposite sides of the room or do not allow them to do a ceremony together. I felt pressured to be apart, but Les and I decided we continually experimented as a couple and wanted to be together. The longer I struggled with negative and paranoid thoughts, the worse my mood became. I had an overpowering urge to run. I typically use running for dealing with overwhelming emotions and laying there being present with myself, and my feelings were beyond uncomfortable. I became terrified I was going to be demon-possessed. *(Please don't laugh. Given my background, this makes perfect sense.)* The fear of dying and going to Hell came roaring back. I decided I had made a mistake and Iboga was a horrible idea. I was never doing this again.

Unfortunately, I became paranoid that the facilitators didn't like me and I wouldn't ask for help. Les realized how badly I was struggling but also knew I had to travel my path. He placed a hand on my arm, always supportive, and encouraged me to talk to the facilitators. I wrestled in my mind until dawn.

When the sky started to lighten, I told the facilitator I wanted to get up and walk around. I shared how my mind was struggling. He explained my brain was purging all of the thoughts that were harming me. Of course, he confirmed my thoughts about them not liking me were untrue. Ironically, one of the times I got up to go to the bathroom, I had some dry heaving, but I never actually threw up. *(Byrd on everything: Throws up. Byrd on Iboga: Doesn't throw up???)* My mind decided to purge with thoughts all night long. As the sky lightened, the dark thoughts eased, and I was so relieved to find my usual positivity returning.

The following day, the intense thoughts came and went in waves. After an hour of crying, I sat down to talk to one of the facilitators. I shared that one of my struggles was that in the background of my soul was this sheer terror of going to Hell. These thoughts had been some of the most overwhelming the night before. As we talked, I identified that my thoughts were not what God would or was saying. God promised never to leave or forsake me. Any separation I felt was my own doing. These untrue beliefs were a considerable part of the mental spiral that would start when I was significantly depressed, growing darker and darker, causing more and more hopelessness, until I decided I had disappointed God, I was a failure, and my only option was to die.

For the first time, I was able to identify the similarity of the thoughts, stop the train of thought, and acknowledge God didn't want me to die. Instead, I remembered and identified my core beliefs about God's indescribable love, grace, and mercy. Les and I discussed the IFS therapy model that our mind creates protectors when we are young, and we can speak to those parts of ourselves. I told my mind that I was safe now. I learned to pull that condemning part of myself close, flooding my mind and heart with love and acceptance. I had a powerful realization that the parts of me that are painful, uncomfortable, or afraid need *more* love. Instead of trying to fight or ignore those parts of myself, I needed to pull them close, listen to the need, and above all, love.

Iboga heightened all of the senses, rewiring every nerve and resulting in increased sensitivity. I could feel the neuroplasticity in my brain. Everything felt new. Experiences, tastes, touch, and sounds were all new. The day after taking Iboga for the first time, we explored sexual experiences together, enjoying the newly intensified sensitivity. It felt like every possible nerve was firing, enhancing sensation in a sexy and gorgeous effect. We spent time touching each other in different ways, slowly and sensuously, loving the escalated connection, openness, and astounding sensation of caressing and being caressed.

As thoughts that showed me hurtful or untrue beliefs about myself would come up, I would mindfully stop and internally discuss what I believed with myself. Each time, I could identify a positive or true belief to replace the unhealthy thoughts. I was truly comfortable with myself for the first time I can remember. My thoughts weren't racing; I didn't feel any pressure to be constantly doing something. I was fully present, calm, and didn't feel the need to distract myself from myself. All of my thoughts settled, leaving peace. We spent days talking, meditating, journaling, reading, and lying in the sun.

Before the first session, the facilitator made a statement that became a powerful belief for me. He said, "You are already whole." I realized I had felt broken for years. Unrepairable. I struggled to live, to continue, knowing past events and people broke me. For the first time, I believed I was whole. He told us our trauma is our wisdom and a gift to others. Our pain and what we experience can benefit and bring healing to others.

When the time came for the second Iboga session, I was nervous. I didn't want to bring up all of those negative thoughts again. On the other hand, the peace and calm on the other side were worth a night of restlessness. I talked to Les and the facilitators, and we agreed to proceed with the following ceremony as a couple. They said few couples could do what we did, but it worked for us.

After we took the medicine and the night started, I was pleasantly surprised to find my thoughts were still calm. I was curled up, comfortable and warm inside my mind. When the facilitator came to check on me, I expressed my surprise and shared my change in mindset and the unhealthy beliefs and thoughts I had let go. He gave me a little more medicine, and I immediately threw up. Afterward, the facilitator remarked how I had spoken about everything I was letting go, and then my body purged. I had no nausea for the rest of the night and felt much better mentally and physically.

During the night, I asked myself if I loved myself. At first, I wasn't sure. After a time, as I sorted out my thoughts and feelings, I realized I did. I pictured every time in my life, at various ages, when I had told myself I hated myself. I went back and hugged myself at each stage and memory. I stood at the altar, frozen in place, marrying my kids' dad. I walked up to my 18-year-old self and hugged myself, stating, "I understand why you made the decision you did, and I forgive you." Instead of feeling the hate and anger for myself that haunted me for decades, I felt acceptance and forgiveness. I led her out of the dark place inside, where she was locked away, crying for so many years. I brought her into the sun and onto the beach in the sunlight to sit with Jesus, finally at peace.

I went back to myself as a young teen, looking in the mirror and hating my body, and I hugged myself. I told myself I was beautiful, perfect at every stage, and *loved*. I told myself I was loved and accepted at every age and stage of life. Afterward, it was like my mind was dancing. I swear I sensed fireworks of flowers and butterflies inside my head, like in a Disney movie. I *loved* myself. I can't remember a time that was true for me in the past.

I worked with the facilitator to do a psychospiritual journey, and together, we processed my thoughts, feelings, and emotions related to many things that were heavy on my soul. She asked when I was diagnosed with Hashimotos, and I told her it was around the time of my second divorce. She asked me to put my hands on my throat and ask myself what I needed. In my mind, I heard the word "forgive." She asked if I needed to forgive myself or someone else. I recognized it was myself I needed to forgive. She asked what I needed to forgive, and everything poured out. Over the next couple of hours, we processed my beliefs about myself as a result of being divorced twice, complicated emotions about what I could have done better as a mother, and my need to connect with God after the ways I had failed and the years of trauma I had experienced. I had no idea all of that was still in there, weighing my soul down and affecting my physical health.

We talked about my guilt related to my children growing up with trauma. I realized the decisions I made over my lifetime were made out of love. I married their dad out of love.

I conceived them out of love. I left out of love. I survived the years of being a single mom out of love.

After sorting through my beliefs about myself as a mother, she gave me a precious gift. She asked me to picture the moon and then imagine a video playing on the moon. I asked my mind to show me the happy memories spent with my children growing up. As I watched the memories play out, I began to cry; there were *so many* of them. I saw the years of laughter and smiles and fun. I had forgotten the thousands of wonderful, loving moments in my heartbreak and misplaced guilt.

While in EMDR, we tried to trace back where my sense of guilt and shame originated. We went as far back as possible, and I couldn't identify a specific time or life event precipitating these feelings. I told my therapist it just seemed always to be there as if I was born with these feelings. How could that be? I couldn't imagine a baby born with these weighty emotions.

During the psychosocial journey, she asked me the same question, and when I came to the same answer, she suggested I look past myself to my matriarchal family line. Shocked, I realized I could see guilt and shame going back from generation to generation to each maternal family member I had known. It finally made sense why I felt like I was born with guilt. We pictured washing generations of my family in God's love, grace, and forgiveness.

We processed each issue that came up until I felt light and clear. I could truly forgive myself, accept myself, and love myself. I was able to forgive others. Like the jellyfish, I can just be. It's not about everything I do. God's indescribable love for me came flooding back, and I reconnected with a lost part of my relationship with God.

After the psychospiritual journey, I lay beside Les, and we both fell asleep. The facilitators later told us very few people can fall asleep during that part of the ceremony, and it's usually people who struggle with chronic, significant sleep issues. I cannot explain the peace in my mind, the unimaginable ability to lay in the dark with myself and my thoughts and be calm. As a result of Iboga, both of us stopped using sleep medication. In preparation for the ceremony, I quit my depression medication altogether, and I was able to remain off the medication after.

All in all, the Iboga treatment was years of EMDR therapy in a single week. Sometimes, my brain even physically hurt like it did after an intense EMDR session. We never delved into specific traumatic events or memories. Instead, Iboga became an amplifier to pull out of my mind all the negative beliefs I had latched onto due to my experiences. I learned to heal my mind by identifying those unhealthy and false beliefs and mindfully replacing each, one by one.

Thoughts from EMDR: January 2024

The one thing I keep coming back to is love. Love God, love others, love yourself.

At last, my kids are grown and on their own. All of us are healing. We are in a good place. Safe homes. I love those not-so-little humans so much.

TODAY, the judge terminated all court orders. I am finally truly free for the first time since I was 16.

I cannot put into words how horrible it has been, how much my soul has longed for a time of peace and to be free. Some days, I didn't think I would make it. A couple of times, I almost didn't.

Today, I say goodbye and close this chapter for good. My younger self made choices I would never make again. I have learned a lot. I can say now the rocky, mountainous desert dirt road with those crazy steep drop-offs has come to a gorgeous place (with the most incredible view, and of course, there's water!).

I turn 40 next month I am determined to move forward in healing, peace, hope, growth, and happiness.

Next up—- a bonfire with 14 years of court documents!!!

And eventually, a fantastic vacation! Maybe on that peaceful island where I dreamed of running away for so long.

I still can't believe I made it through. My soul is breathing a sigh of relief. My heart is lighter.

Takeaways

I can't explain everything, but plant medicine is incredibly effective and should utilized with a trained guide. Looking back, I wonder if my mushroom experience would have been different with someone to guide me when my mind became dark.

As time went by after the Iboga, I noticed several long-term changes:
-Able to fall asleep and stay asleep without medication
-Experiencing deep, calm sleep with decreased restlessness at night

-No need for depression medication, and depression has not returned

-No more physical pain in my hip, lower back

-Self-love and acceptance

-Openness to others and new experiences, more empathy

-Interact with others without feeling emotionally exhausted and drained after

-Much busier socially without feeling overwhelmed, more of myself to give to others

-Comfortable in my head and with myself, able to be alone with myself and my thoughts

-Decreased feelings of being "bored" and don't feel the need to distract myself

-Less TV watching

-Increased feeling of peace internally

-No more ADHD symptoms like my mind is jumping chaotically here, there, and everywhere

-Able to go into grocery stores and remain calm inside; do not dread going into stores anymore

-Able to look at pictures from the past with calm and acceptance, without feeling shame or self-hatred, and do not feel sad or depressed afterward

-I forgive myself and others

-Able to lay in bed at night without racing thoughts

-No racing thoughts during the day, improved focus

-Able to identify and change unhealthy thoughts and beliefs

-Increased purpose and direction

-I am whole

-Controlled eating habits without food noise, less urge to snack on junk food, and less urge to eat sweets

-Able to meditate with a calm mind

-Able to be fully present

-Decreased feeling of pressure to be constantly busy or to perform

-Intense triggers related to the smell of alcohol are just *gone*

Les's Story

Iboga changed me forever. I am not the same Les who existed before Iboga. That is not to say that the Les I am now didn't exist, only that he was shrouded and hamstrung by beliefs that weren't serving me. I spent two years working with psychedelics to heal from the wounds of my past, but despite all of that work, I believed I was broken and needed healing. Remember my encounters with the Earth Mother? Yup, she told me I needed to heal, too. What the Bwiti traditions taught me was that my trauma was not what needed healing. My past was my wisdom, but the errant beliefs I carried from those experiences were what I needed to heal.

In the West, we believe that we have to *fix* our trauma. To face it and change our perceptions of it. The Bwiti teaches people that their trauma is not what is essential. What is important is what you believe about yourself. Iboga gives you the ability to address your beliefs. This thought process was revolutionary for me.

Iboga is more than something that can open your mind and allow you to edit your beliefs. Iboga is also a medicine that dives into every part of your body, quietly cleaning out every part of you.

Over the past 20 years, I have struggled with profound insomnia. I have taken just about every pharmaceutical and non-pharmaceutical sedative and sleep medication. In the months leading up to the retreat, my sleep was at an all-time low, leaving me on the brink of insanity. I felt as if I was one or two nights away from losing my mind. Our prep for the retreat included instructions not to bring any sleep medicine, if applicable. I was extremely hesitant, but I left them at home. *(While also rolling a few joints to bring along, just in case).*

Our first Iboga medicine ceremony was on the day we arrived for the retreat. We expected we wouldn't sleep until the next night due to the stimulating effects of Iboga. As we settled onto our mats and put on our eye masks, the facilitator's final words were, "You are already whole." Those words rang through my mind for the whole night. Am I already whole? What would that look like?

With this mantra, I journeyed through my life's healing pathways, seeing where I had healed from past traumas. I realized I was carrying this deeply held belief that I was not whole. I could never repair my cracks and missing pieces. I wondered whether I could change this belief at the end of this journey. Could I switch from "I am broken" to "I am already whole?" *I did.* And my whole being altered with that one change.

I pondered my decades-long sleep issues. I assessed my beliefs about sleep and found that my beliefs around sleep were that I would never sleep well again. I removed that belief and installed a new one. And guess what? I haven't taken anything for sleep since. I sleep 4 to 6 hours each night and wake energetic and rested. Prior to the retreat, I was tracking my sleep with a wearable sleep tracker. I discovered that my sleep, prior to Iboga, was very low in REM cycle sleep (5% or so most nights). After the retreat, my REM cycle percentage increased to 15-20%. If I need extra sleep, I can nap or catch an extra hour the next night. If I wake up at 2 a.m., I don't freak out. I know I will get what rest I need. Twenty years of insomnia with nightly anxiety and fear, and it was all washed away in a night.

The medicine fixed my insomnia and the belief that I was broken. Was that all? Nope. I have struggled for years with an upper back injury that causes searing nerve-like shooting pain to lance between my shoulder blades. Like my insomnia, the pain in my back was worse than ever. Right before the retreat, I shared with Byrd that I am in significant pain daily. She was shocked to hear that it was so bad. My pain would be a constant 4 out of 10, with multiple spikes of 6 to 8 out of 10 throughout the day and night.

Following the first Iboga treatment, Byrd and I laid out under the sun for most of the day. I sat cross-legged or lay on the hard ground for hours. After about 3 hours, I noticed my back felt tight. Then, it dawned on me that I hadn't felt discomfort in my back since the ceremony. The pain was gone. I quickly stretched, and my back loosened up and returned to normal. Since the ceremony? The pain is still gone—no pain while sleeping or during the day. If my back gets stiff from an awkward position or sitting too long, I can stretch it out.

It is miraculous how different I feel after Iboga. I am full of life force, sleeping at night, and pain-free. I have an enhanced energy and drive to help others. Before, my energy was so low that paying my bills and going to work was too much. Now? I can work for hours and engage with friends and family, and I still feel like I have more to give.

Iboga is the most potent medicine I have ever encountered. After our retreat, we have inadvertently become Iboga apostles. At every turn, we find another person who could have their life changed by this medicine. We hope to work with Iboga more in the coming years, but we can spread the good word in the meantime.

After the first ceremony, Byrd and I went to our room to lie down and rest. One thing led to the other *(as usual for us)*, and we started touching each other. Wow! My nerves, and hers by her report, were hypersensitive. I felt as if I had never been caressed before, with sensations multiplied by many times. When touching Byrd, I explored her body as if it were new to me, feeling every curve, corner, and crevice. The sensations of intercourse were overwhelming and amazing. The orgasm? Phenomenal! I don't know if this is normal on Iboga, but our experience makes us wonder. If you and your partner participate in an Iboga ceremony, sneak off afterward for some intimate couple time. I hope you experience what we did.

How to Safely Use the Dark Web: Baby Steps

Finding psychedelics, for most of us, is very challenging to do safely. Our initial experiences were a result of growing psilocybin mushrooms or finding friends of friends who know a street pharmacist. We had always heard that these things were widely available on the "Dark Web," but we had no idea where to find this "Dark Web." Les began to search for the Dark Web, hoping to find a source for psychedelics.

The Dark Web consists of websites that are only accessible using specific web browsers. One cannot use Google to find websites on the Dark Web. The Dark Web is best known for its illegal activities. However, it is also used extensively in countries with severe internet censorship or restrictions to discuss political and other prohibited subjects. The Dark Web is designed to protect users' privacy, but you must set up specific systems to ensure your privacy and safety.

 Should you choose to access the Dark Web, do a lot of research. The complete guide on Dark Web security is the DarkNet Bible, and a copy can be found linked in this Reddit forum's FAQs (follow the QR code). You can also find printed copies of the DarkNet Bible online. Also, Reddit is an excellent resource for answering all your questions about the Dark Web. You can use many layers of security, and your research will help you determine what level of protection is right for you.

A FEW FINAL THOUGHTS

One tradition we learned during our Iboga retreat was the practice of performing the Saint Francis of Assisi Twin Hearts for Psychological Healing meditation after any use of psychedelics. At the end of our six-day retreat, the facilitator played this meditation as the last activity before leaving, and we all joined in. He explained that using psychedelics makes you sensitive to outside influences, and this helps ground you before returning to day-to-day life. We understand there are many beliefs surrounding practices such as meditation. However, we found it a meaningful way to end an experience together in mental calmness and peace. Follow the QR code to try the Twin Hearts meditation out for yourself.

The Mediation on Twin Hearts includes blessing the world to alleviate suffering and praying for society's well-being. The meditation focuses on loving kindness, self-healing imagery, and open awareness. [44] We are sharing the method developed by Master Choa Kok Sui as this version is specifically for psychological healing, the aspect of the self most impacted by the use of psychedelics. This meditation enhances your physical, mental, emotional, and spiritual well-being. [45] Couples can focus on sending each other, or loved ones, loving-kindness in addition to the whole world.

Overall, these past years of experimenting, learning, and growing with psychedelics dramatically changed our lives. We went from broken and wounded souls to living vibrant, loving, and full lives. "[Psychedelics] don't mean anything unless they change what you do in your life." [66] We hope you can learn from our trials *(and sometimes errors)* and find your paths to healing. There is so much hurt in the world, and it is our hope this knowledge will bring some healing. Psychedelics are the future of mental health treatment, and once we knew how powerful these medicines are, we wanted to share this knowledge with other couples.

It is possible to heal without diving into episodes of trauma over and over for years. People can recover from trauma without talking about it. [65, pg 255] And while sometimes healing requires revisiting the past, it's more important to address the unhealthy beliefs resulting from the trauma rather than rehashing the details of the trauma itself. We have many medications for the body, but not many medicines that can genuinely help us heal the mind and soul. Psychedelics bypass those barriers we erect to protect ourselves and allow us to access our deep inner parts.

We realize psychedelics aren't for everyone, but these tools can help many. As Anne Shulgin described it, "[Psychedelics] are tools for anyone who's on any kind of spiritual journey." [66] The research is growing by the day. We encourage everyone to continue their own learning and independent education. Talk to others. Consult a medical provider or mental health professional to discuss specifics unique to your situation. Discover what works for you and your partner. Above all, maintain an open mind.

We learned that our minds and souls want to heal, and you and your partner have the capability to help and support each other on this unique journey. Often, couples want to do better but need help with the *how*. We hope this gives you some tools to work with.

"All great changes are preceded by chaos. The disruption we see in the world is the prelude to emergence. Let's all commit to a more peaceful, just, sustainable, healthier, and happier world. We must become what we wish to see by transcending our limited tribal identities." [63]

BEFORE YOU TRIP CHECKLIST:

For more details, refer to the chapter on The 3 S's of Tripping: Set, Setting, and Surrender

- **Is your partner safe to trip with?**

- **Check-in with each other - is now a good time for both of you to trip?**

- **Identify a comfortable, secure, and safe setting where both of you are comfortable**

- **Blankets, pillows, sleeping bags, etc.**

- **Tasty snacks and treats**

- **Drinks**

- **Electrolytes**

- **Speaker and Playlist of your favs as a couple**

- **Start with sharing intentions out loud**

- **While feeling deeper connection and openness, make time to check in about any problematic issues you would like to discuss**

- **End with the Twin Hearts for Psychological Healing meditation**

Special Note: Most standard Urine Drug Screens do not test for psychedelics. However, there is the chance MDMA or MDA might cause a false positive for amphetamines.

If you are concerned about potential testing, allow 2-4 days for these medicines to clear your system.

RESOURCES

Psychedelic consultation appointments with Les and Byrd:

www.couplesguidetopsychedelics.com

MAPS Psychedelic Support Hotline: 623-473-7433

Saint Francis of Assis Twin Hearts Meditation:

Recorded Meditation

Written Meditation

Where to Purchase Testing Kits:

Whether you are sourcing medicine from the Dark Web directly or from a trusted friend, you *must* test it for fentanyl, at the very least. We recommend testing to verify the substance you have as well. Testing is essential for your safety. For example, MDA is about twice as potent per milligram as MDMA, and mistaking MDA for MDMA could result in taking *way* too much and result in potentially unsafe or uncomfortable experiences.

So, you now realize you need to purchase some testing kits. Right? Good. The internet has many companies offering reagent testing kits, and everyone has their favorites. We have had positive experiences with the first listed below, but that doesn't make it the best or only option.

TN Scientific: This is our preferred testing company. TN is highly regarded in the psychedelics community, and their customer service is excellent. We own several of their kits, so we can test for fentanyl and differentiate between substances. The kits are affordable and very easy to use.

Dance Safe: Dance Safe is a highly regarded, non-profit organization that provides harm-reduction education and services online and at festivals. Their testing kits are affordable, and you are supporting a great organization.

Whatever company you choose, research to ensure they provide quality testing supplies and watch their videos on how to use the kits properly.

Recommended Books

"How to Change Your Mind" by Michael Pollan

"The Body Keeps the Score: Brain, Mind, and Body in the Healing of Trauma" by Bessel van der Kolk M.D.

"The Great Sex Rescue" by Sheila Gregoire

Recommended Podcasts

Alt Med- *"An introduction to Ibogaine: Troy Valencia"*

No Fallen Heroes- *"Bridging the Gap Between Science and Healing"*

Living Indubiously- *"Sienna Burton, a Missoko Bwiti Initiated Iboga Medicine Provider"*

Recommended Documentaries

"How to Change Your Mind" Netflix documentary series

Trip Videos

(Note: We like to pick our own music while watching the videos.)

Mushroom Trippy Video

Nexus 65: Dark Forest

Electric Samurai

Escape Reality

ACKNOWLEDGMENTS

We would be nothing without those who love us deeply. Special love to our children S. "my baby girl," R. "my little man," I. "oldest daughter," C. "youngest daughter," and S. "our adopted child" – all of you are our heart and soul. Words can never say a big enough thank you to Byrd's family- parents P.&S., brother and his beautiful wife J.&C., brother M., lovely sister and niece J.&J., grandparents P.&J., uncles R.&R., cuz Z.R., brother and his beautiful partner S.&C., and extended family G. You kept us going too many times to count! Helping out in a million practical ways and just listening when there was no way to fix it. The ideas in this book are not reflective of your opinions, but we are grateful you love us anyway.

We want to give a very special mention to Byrd's Grandma C.C.. I only hope you can see that I'm ok now. I made it back to the sunlight, just like you thought I would. You would love to hear all these stories. I love you so much; thank you for all the times you were there for me. You instilled the love of writing in me going way back.

Thank you to our closest friends G.C., H.K., R.A., C.N., P.N. & C.N., T.G., and C.A.& J.B. You guys were the first to hear about our explorations, the idea for the book, and the first to volunteer to read our manuscript that day we finished writing while watching the sunset in Cancun. You have filled the years with laughter and become the family we chose. Your wisdom, support, and feedback are invaluable.

A debt of gratitude to those who read our book in advance and provided feedback and guidance on publishing: D.B., Z.R., D.T., M.S., R.A., R.D., and T.G.. You guys are part of the friends and family categories, too - but deserved special recognition for your editorial roles!

Shout out to our work colleagues. We cannot name all of you, but please know that we appreciate growing together as professionals. You care for patients and each other day in and out, bringing healing and compassion in the lowest moments.

Special mention from Byrd to each of my amazing running friends (there are too many of you to name individually!). When times were dark, you hit me up to run on our favorite trails, which meant the world. You introduced me to the ultra-running community and showed me physical feats I never thought were possible. I cannot say how much I enjoy every one of our memories and miles together (even the uphills!).

Written with so much love for every one of you!

REFERENCES

1. Smith H. (2000). Cleansing the Doors of Perception: The Religious Significance of Entheogenic Plants and Chemicals. New York, New York: Jeremy P. Tarcher/Putnam. p. 101. ISBN 978-1-58542-034-6.

2. Cohen, I. V., Makunts, T., Abagyan, R., & Thomas, K. (2021). Concomitant drugs associated with increased mortality for MDMA users reported in a drug safety surveillance database. Scientific reports, 11(1), 5997.

3. Grob, C. S., & Grigsby, J. (Eds.). (2021). Handbook of medical hallucinogens. Guilford Publications.

4. Baggott, M. J., Garrison, K. J., Coyle, J. R., Galloway, G. P., Barnes, A. J., Huestis, M. A., & Mendelson, J. E. (2019). Effects of the psychedelic amphetamine MDA (3, 4-methylenedioxyamphetamine) in healthy volunteers. Journal of Psychoactive Drugs, 51(2), 108-117.

5. Shulgin, A. T., & Shulgin, A. (1991). PIHKAL: a chemical love story (Vol. 963009605). Berkeley, CA: Transform Press.

6. Davis WM, Hatoum HT, Waters IW. Toxicity of MDA (3,4-methylenedioxyamphetamine) considered for relevance to hazards of MDMA (Ecstasy) abuse. Alcohol Drug Res. 1987;7(3):123-34. PMID: 2881551.

7. Passie, T., Halpern, J. H., Stichtenoth, D. O., Emrich, H. M., & Hintzen, A. (2008). The pharmacology of lysergic acid diethylamide: a review. CNS neuro-

science & therapeutics, 14(4), 295-314.

8. Smith, D. E., Raswyck, G. E., & Dickerson Davidson, L. (2014). From Hofmann to the Haight Ashbury, and into the future: the past and potential of lysergic acid diethylamide. Journal of Psychoactive Drugs, 46(1), 3-10.

9. Ketchum, J. S., & Ketchum, J. S. (2012). Chemical warfare secrets almost forgotten. WestBow Press.

10. Passie, T., Halpern, J. H., Stichtenoth, D. O., Emrich, H. M., & Hintzen, A. (2008). The pharmacology of lysergic acid diethylamide: a review. CNS neuroscience & therapeutics, 14(4), 295-314.

11. Holze, F., Gasser, P., Müller, F., Dolder, P. C., & Liechti, M. E. (2023). Lysergic acid diethylamide–assisted therapy in patients with anxiety with and without a life-threatening illness: a randomized, double-blind, placebo-controlled phase II study. Biological Psychiatry, 93(3), 215-223.

12. Jelen, L. A., & Stone, J. M. (2021). Ketamine for depression. International Review of Psychiatry, 33(3), 207-228.

13. Kim, J. W., Suzuki, K., Kavalali, E. T., & Monteggia, L. M. (2023). Ketamine: mechanisms and relevance to treatment of depression. Annual review of medicine, 75.

14. Krupitsky, E. M., Burakov, A. M., Dunaevsky, I. V., Romanova, T. N., Slavina, T. Y., & Grinenko, A. Y. (2007). Single versus repeated sessions of ketamine-assisted psychotherapy for people with heroin dependence. Journal of psychoactive drugs, 39(1), 13-19.

15. Srirangam, S., & Mercer, J. (2012). Ketamine bladder syndrome: an important differential diagnosis when assessing a patient with persistent lower urinary tract symptoms. Case Reports, 2012, bcr2012006447.

16. González, D., Torrens, M., & Farré, M. (2015). Acute effects of the novel psychoactive drug 2C-B on emotions. BioMed research international, 2015.

17. Shulgin, A. T., & Shulgin, A. (1991). PIHKAL: a chemical love story (Vol.

963009605). Berkeley, CA: Transform Press.

18. Hartogsohn, I. (2017). Constructing drug effects: A history of set and setting. Drug Science, Policy and Law, 3, 2050324516683325.

19. Aday, J. S., Davis, A. K., Mitzkovitz, C. M., Bloesch, E. K., & Davoli, C. C. (2021). Predicting reactions to psychedelic drugs: A systematic review of states and traits related to acute drug effects. ACS Pharmacology & Translational Science, 4(2), 424-435.

20. Russ, S. L., Carhart-Harris, R. L., Maruyama, G., & Elliott, M. S. (2019). States and traits related to the quality and consequences of psychedelic experiences. Psychology of Consciousness: Theory, Research, and Practice, 6(1), 1.

21. https://coraliesawruk.medium.com/why-setting-intentions-is-the-way-to-achieve-your-goals-76d5e026d5d5

22. https://www.change.org/p/my-brother-was-sentenced-to-life-without-parole-for-a-nonviolent-drug-offense

23. https://www.washingtonpost.com/news/post-nation/wp/2016/08/30/obama-commutes-sentences-of-111-inmates-setting-record-for-a-single-month/

24. https://en.wikipedia.org/wiki/Timothy_L._Tyler

25. https://erowid.org/culture/characters/hanna_jon/hanna_jon_article1_free_lsd_three.pdf

26. https://www.change.org/p/clemency-for-robert-j-riley-life-in-prison-for-a-non violent-drug-offens

27. https://www.indiegogo.com/projects/psychedelic-awareness-clemency-for-lsd-pows#/

28. https://www.dea.gov/sites/default/files/pubs/states/newsrel/sanfran112403.html

29. https://en.wikipedia.org/wiki/William_Leonard_Pickard#cite_note-hausfeld-15

30. https://www.nationalgeographic.com/animals/article/ibogaine-pschedelic-dr
    ug-root-fair-trade-gabon

31. https://www.newportacademy.com/resources/substance-abuse/ayahuasca/

32. Frecska, E., Bokor, P., & Winkelman, M. (2016). The therapeutic potentials of
    ayahuasca: possible effects against various diseases of civilization. Frontiers in
    pharmacology, 7, 35.

33. Dinis-Oliveira, R. J., Pereira, C. L., & da Silva, D. D. (2019). Pharmacokinetic
    and pharmacodynamic aspects of peyote and mescaline: clinical and forensic
    repercussions. Current molecular pharmacology, 12(3), 184-194.

34. Doesburg-van Kleffens, M., Zimmermann-Klemd, A. M., & Gründemann, C.
    (2023). An Overview on the Hallucinogenic Peyote and Its Alkaloid Mescaline:
    The Importance of Context, Ceremony and Culture. Molecules, 28(24), 7942.

35. https://doubleblindmag.com/ibogaine-and-iboga/

36. Davis, A. K., Averill, L. A., Sepeda, N. D., Barsuglia, J. P., & Amoroso, T.
    (2020). Psychedelic treatment for trauma-related psychological and cognitive
    impairment among US special operations forces veterans. Chronic Stress, 4,
    2470547020939564.

37. https://med.stanford.edu/news/all-news/2024/01/ibogaine-ptsd.html

38. https://en.wikipedia.org/wiki/Legal_status_of_ayahuasca_by_country#:~:text
    =Ayahuasca%20typically%20contains%20DMT%2C%20a,law%20also%20typi
    cally%20outlaws%20DMT

39. https://psychonautwiki.org/wiki/2C-B#Dangerous_interactions

40. Guidance, R., Recalls, P., Reporting, S., Medicines, U., Medicines, I., Update,
    P., ... & Statements, D. G. (2007). Serious reactions with tramadol: seizures and
    serotonin syndrome. Prescriber Update, 28(1), 11-13.

41. Nayak, S. M., Gukasyan, N., Barrett, F. S., Erowid, E., & Griffiths, R. R.
    (2021). Classic psychedelic coadministration with lithium, but not lamotrigine,
    is associated with seizures: an analysis of online psychedelic experience reports.

Pharmacopsychiatry, 54(05), 240-245.

42. Silins, E., Copeland, J., & Dillon, P. (2007). Qualitative review of serotonin syndrome, ecstasy (MDMA) and the use of other serotonergic substances: hierarchy of risk. Australian & New Zealand Journal of Psychiatry, 41(8), 649-655.

43. Makunts, T., Jerome, L., Abagyan, R., & de Boer, A. (2022). Reported cases of serotonin syndrome in MDMA users in FAERS database. Frontiers in Psychiatry, 12, 824288.

44. Meena, B. M., Manasa, B., Vijayakumar, V., Salagame, K. K. K., & Jois, S. N. (2021). Nursing student's experiences of meditation on twin hearts during eight weeks practice: A qualitative content analysis. SAGE Open Nursing, 7, 23779608211052118.

45. http://www.bahaistudies.net/asma/twinhearts.pdf

46. Straumann, I., Ley, L., Holze, F., Becker, A. M., Klaiber, A., Wey, K., ... & Liechti, M. E. (2023). Acute effects of MDMA and LSD co-administration in a double-blind placebo-controlled study in healthy participants. Neuropsychopharmacology, 1-9.

47. Schechter, M. D. (1998). Candyflipping': synergistic discriminative effect of LSD and MDMA. European journal of pharmacology, 341(2-3), 131-134.

48. https://en.wikipedia.org/wiki/Psilocybin_mushroom

49. Schwartz, R. (2023). No bad parts: Healing trauma & restoring wholeness with the internal family systems model. Random House.

50. Schwartz, R. (2023). Introduction to internal family systems.

51. Zuccato, C., & Cattaneo, E. (2009). Brain-derived neurotrophic factor in neurodegenerative diseases. Nature Reviews Neurology, 5(6), 311-322.

52. Moliner, R., Girych, M., Brunello, C. A., Kovaleva, V., Biojone, C., Enkavi, G., ... & Castrén, E. (2023). Psychedelics promote plasticity by directly binding to BDNF receptor TrkB. Nature Neuroscience, 26(6), 1032-1041.

53. Calder, A. E., & Hasler, G. (2023). Towards an understanding of psychedelic-induced neuroplasticity. Neuropsychopharmacology, 48(1), 104-112.

54. https://www.amazon.com/Great-Sex-Rescue-Recover-Intended/dp/1540900827

55. Kopra, E. I., Ferris, J. A., Winstock, A. R., Young, A. H., & Rucker, J. J. (2022). Adverse experiences resulting in emergency medical treatment following the use of magic mushrooms. Journal of Psychopharmacology, 36(8), 965-973.

56. Smith, K. W., Sicignano, D. J., Hernandez, A. V., & White, C. M. (2022). MDMA-assisted psychotherapy for treatment of posttraumatic stress disorder: A systematic review with meta-analysis. The Journal of Clinical Pharmacology, 62(4), 463-471.

57. https://maps.org/mdma/

58. An, D., Wei, C., Wang, J., & Wu, A. (2021). Intranasal ketamine for depression in adults: a systematic review and meta-analysis of randomized, double-blind, placebo-controlled trials. Frontiers in psychology, 12, 648691.

59. Clements, J. A., Nimmo, W. S., & Grant, I. S. (1982). Bioavailability, pharmacokinetics, and analgesic activity of ketamine in humans. Journal of pharmaceutical sciences, 71(5), 539-542.

60. https://www.ketamineacademy.com/post/ketamine-administration-routes-at-a-glance-a-quick-comparison-for-clinicians-on-the-go

61. https://doubleblindmag.com/mushrooms/tripping-combining-drugs/jedi-flipping-shrooms-acid-and-molly/

62. Galvão-Coelho, N. L., Marx, W., Gonzalez, M., Sinclair, J., de Manincor, M., Perkins, D., & Sarris, J. (2021). Classic serotonergic psychedelics for mood and depressive symptoms: a meta-analysis of mood disorder patients and healthy participants. Psychopharmacology, 238, 341-354.

63. https://twitter.com/DeepakChopra/status/1013402730537340929?lang=en

64. Lesch, K. P. (2004). Gene-environment interaction and the genetics of depres-

sion. Journal of Psychiatry and Neuroscience, 29(3), 174-184.

65. Van der Kolk, B. A. (2014). The body keeps the score: brain, mind, and body in the healing of trauma. New York, Viking.

66. 2010. Dirty Pictures. Prairie Coast Films. Shaul, Shaun Patrick.